Whereas the Bible talks abou ... the power of God. The cen ... *Prayer* is this: GOD HAS TH ... in a biblically astute manner, present a topic that should not be ignored by the church. This book is both practical and thought provoking. A "must" read for anyone who wants to know more about God as Healer.

Dr. Jim "Umfundisi" Lo
Professor of Religion, Campus Pastor - Intercessor
Indiana Wesleyan University (Marion, IN)
Assistant District Superintendent
Indiana North District of The Wesleyan Church

This book provides biblical clarity the church desperately needs regarding our mandate and call to be the healing hands of Jesus in our hurting world. It addresses the questions and concerns surrounding the topic of healing from a sound biblical base partnered with years of experience. These writers share from the frontlines of ministry. I praise the Lord for His blessing upon Wellsprings of Freedom International, as they equip the local church with tools needed to minister effectively.

Rev. Lexa Ennis
Co-Pastor
Broadview Wesleyan Church (Broadview, IL)

I am excited about this ministry, after traveling to Wellsprings of Freedom International and participating in two physical healing prayer sessions and seeing what God is doing for His people! With the support of Pastor Mike Ennis Sr., we added this healing ministry to our local Wellsprings of Freedom team. Lives are being changed at The River! Thanks to Lynette Johnson and Brian Burke for your insight and leadership in this ministry.

Ronald Smith
Healing Team Leader
The River, A Wesleyan Church (Frankford, DE)

THE
POWER
OF
HEALING
PRAYER

A MANUAL FOR PHYSICAL HEALING PRAYER

BRIAN S. BURKE

WITH LYNETTE JOHNSON

PRESS

Nashville, TN

The Power of Healing Prayer: A Manual for Physical Healing Prayer
Brian S. Burke with Lynette Johnson
All rights reserved.

Front Cover Design by: Caleb Hensley
Interior Design by Pine Hill Graphics

Copyright © 2016 Wellsprings of Freedom International

Published by ACW Press
PO Box 110390
Nashville, Tennessee 37222
www.acwpress.com

The views expressed or implied in this work do not necessarily reflect those of ACW Press. Ultimate design, content, and editorial accuracy of this work is the responsibility of the author(s).

ISBN 978-1-934668-67-2

Printed in the United States of America.

Acknowledgements

It is with a heart filled with gratitude that I would like to take a moment to thank my wife, Cara, and my family, for their love and ongoing support. I also want to thank Rev. Tim Howard, Lynette Johnson, and our army of more than 125 volunteers who faithfully serve at Wellsprings of Freedom International in Rock Island, Illinois, on a regular basis. A special thanks goes out to Dawn, Jenny, Tammy, Gretchen, Connie, Sharon, Cathy, Ann, Lisa, Rosie, Sheri, and Lynn, for their time, sacrifice, and ongoing investment in the physical healing prayer sessions. Your love, compassion, gentleness, and sacrifice has touched hundreds of lives over the last few years. Thank you for your servants' hearts and for allowing the Lord to use you as instruments of healing to those who are suffering. All glory to the God of miracles for the great things He has done in and through the Wellsprings of Freedom ministry.

Rev. Brian S. Burke

I would also like to take this opportunity to thank the current physical healing team members: Tammy Schaver, Dawn DeGaris, Jenny Farrell, Connie Whan, Gretchen Hans, Sharon Deadmond, Cathy Loose, Ann Zullo, Rosie Baker, Lynn Gustafson, Lisa Soto, and Sheri Holgersson. It is because of your love and dedication to see others be healed and set free that many received their healing. A special thank you to Steve and Susan Painter, who were instrumental in the beginning of this ministry with the many hours we spent in prayer. Thank you to Rev. Tim Howard and Rev. Brian Burke for your guidance, encouragement, and affirmation.

Lynette Johnson

Table of Contents

Foreword

One of the things I most appreciate about freedom ministry is how God shows up and does amazing things. Miraculous things would be a more accurate description. As the founder of Wellsprings of Freedom International, I have the privilege of hearing firsthand many of the amazing testimonies told by the people who are coming to our facility for physical healing prayer. In His Word, the Lord tells us that He has given us authority to heal the sick and drive out demons. I wonder how many of us have actually observed a miraculous healing or even witnessed a demon being cast out? In our heart of hearts, we long to see miracles, and yet we find ourselves stuck in the middle of a faith gap. We want to believe in miracles, but I think we are hesitant to step out in faith due to our own doubt and fear that it won't work. The fear of praying for a miraculous healing to occur and nothing happening keeps us paralyzed from trying.

Many of us have to see things with our own eyes in order to believe. I personally struggled with the concept of casting out demons until I had an actual encounter with one. Once I saw the reality of it with my own eyes, I believed. A couple of years later, I witnessed another kind of miracle, a physical healing! I was visiting a friend in the hospital whose bowels were completely paralyzed. She had been this way for a couple of days and the doctors didn't know what they were going to do. She asked me if I would please pray for her and I did. I gently placed two fingertips on the side of her arm and prayed for God to bring healing to her paralyzed bowels. In the middle of my prayer, she interrupted me and told me I needed to leave right away. With a serious look on her face, she said, "I'm not kidding, please go now." I left her room troubled, not completely understanding what had just happened. It wasn't until an hour or so later that she called me to tell me why I had to leave so quickly. She told me that the second my fingers touched her arm, a shock of energy flooded through her body. She went on to tell me that her bowels instantaneously came alive. Two sentences into my prayer she needed to use the restroom in a hurry! It was because of this experience that I began to pray with greater boldness and confidence for physical healing.

For whatever reason, God chose to allow me to see that physical healing is still possible today. But what about the many believers who find themselves experiencing a similar faith gap? How can they bridge the gap and walk out their faith in a more biblical, experiential, and balanced way?

I believe the book you now have in your hands is the answer. It is one thing to write about theory or hypothesize ideas on how to pray with more boldness. This book, however, has been written from years of hands-on experience. Brian and Lynette have both experienced firsthand the reality of praying over someone for physical healing and watching God answer their prayers. But they are not content to keep what they have learned to themselves. They have partnered together to write this training manual on physical healing prayer. It is filled with true stories of miraculous healing, step-by-step instructions for how to lead physical healing prayer sessions, biblical support for healing prayer, and a healthy balanced explanation for why God sometimes chooses not to heal.

Perhaps you have felt led to pray with more boldness, but simply did not know how. Get ready, because that's about to change. By applying the concepts of this book, you will be encouraged to step more boldly into prayer and be equipped to launch a new prayer ministry in your church!

Rev. Tim Howard
Founder and President, Wellsprings of Freedom International

Preface

I (Lynette) was born and raised in Geneseo, Illinois. I was saved at a vacation Bible school program that my aunt took me to when I was eleven years old. I wasn't quite sure what had happened at that time. I went to church every week and Sunday school until I was seventeen years old. I didn't attend church much after that, except on holidays, until I was in my early thirties. At this time, I was in a crisis and nothing seemed to be working out in my life. I just happened to be watching a program where a TV preacher was giving the salvation message, and received Jesus as my Lord and Savior. My life was dramatically changed from that point on.

I was in my first year of an RN nursing program. I always felt I had compassion for those who were sick, and nursing seemed to be a good fit for me. At this same time, I served in my church as a deacon and Christian Education Director. I was the junior and senior high youth leader, and led Sunday school classes for junior and senior high school students and adults. I wanted all God had for me and I wanted to do what He said I could do.

While I was still a student nurse, I was asked to privately sit with a patient who was in the ICU and dying. The patient had a serious heart condition and was blind and deaf. I asked the Lord how I was to communicate with someone who couldn't see or hear me and seemed to be unconscious. I sensed that He wanted me to gently lay my hands on the person as I prayed for healing and read and declared scriptures over their body. To my surprise, the patient later asked to be taken to church! I shared this news with the family when they returned and they looked at me like I was crazy. The following week, the floor nurse who had been on duty that day when I privately sat with the patient asked me if I had healed that person, because the patient got better and was discharged home! I was stunned to say the least. Jesus had healed the patient.

I saw on television some miracles happening at healing crusades across the USA, and kept asking the Lord if that was for real. I had to find out. So I went to several healing crusades that drew thousands of people where I witnessed the healing power of God in a corporate setting as hundreds were healed and gave their personal testimonies. I received my answer. God healed me of chronic pain that I had after I had a tumor removed several years before. All the pain was gone and it has never returned.

Over the years, I have had numerous opportunities to pray for people to be healed and have seen miracles happen at times. I led a weekly prayer group in my home for seven years. We prayed about everything and saw some amazing answers to prayer. My own sister was struggling with infertility, and after several rounds of fertility drugs, was not able to get pregnant. As a last resort, she asked for healing prayer. God answered her prayer and she had a baby boy! A couple of years later, she was trying to get pregnant again, with the same results as before, and came to us again for prayer. She got pregnant a second time and had another boy.

I was also a part of the spiritual warfare ministry (TLC was the original name of the ministry back then) at Heritage Church in Rock Island, Illinois. At this time, I was serving as an Intercessor on two teams. I took every opportunity to pray for the sick and was involved with the healing prayer teams at Heritage. I wanted to do the works that Jesus said we could do (John 14:12).

A few years later, I was babysitting for my infant great-granddaughter. Her mom told me that the baby had a hernia the doctor said would require surgical repair. I said to myself, "no way." I didn't want this little baby to go through surgery. So I checked her out, and sure enough, she had an umbilical hernia that stood out one-half to three-quarters of an inch. I laid my hand gently on the hernia and commanded it in the name of Jesus to go back in where it belonged. I didn't see anything happen at the time and just went on with my day. A couple of days later I was babysitting her again, and when I changed her diaper I noticed that the hernia was gone!

In 2013, I went on a mission trip with Wellsprings of Freedom International. On these trips we have host families who normally open their homes to us and give us a comfortable place to sleep. The hostess I was staying with was having a problem with chronic pain from fibromyalgia. I asked her if she wanted prayer for that and she gladly accepted. The pain left after prayer from another team member and myself. The next morning, our hostess was filled with joy as she danced and jumped around the kitchen! She reported that she had no pain anywhere in her body. I couldn't wait to tell the rest of the team what had just happened.

On the way home from this mission trip, a team member asked for prayer for a painful knee. As we prayed, I put my hand gently on her knee. During that prayer time, I felt the bone under my hand shift. The team member reported that all the pain was gone!

Shortly after that mission trip, Pastor Tim Howard asked me to put together and lead a physical healing prayer team. I was already serving as a team member in the freedom sessions for many years and was asked to step out of these sessions to lead the physical healing prayer sessions. When we launched that first healing prayer session, I knew I had just stepped into what God had created me to do. I could see how He had been preparing me for this all along the way. It is truly amazing to see what God is doing. He is amazing!

Why We Started the Physical Healing Prayer Sessions

When I was young, I (Brian) had the honor and privilege of growing up in the midst of an exciting church plant in northern New Jersey. When our family got connected to this new (Wesleyan) church, we met inside my high school cafeteria for weekend worship services. Although the church was only able to rent a small office space at the time, there was a great deal of excitement, energy, and enthusiasm for what God was doing in our midst. Nonbelievers were coming to faith and finding new life in Christ and new believers were being discipled. We were beginning to engage our community with the life-changing power of Jesus Christ.

As small as we were as a new church plant, we watched the Holy Spirit move powerfully among us. I vividly remember our Wednesday evening prayer meetings and special prayer vigils that we occasionally held for those who were battling cancer and struggling with various physical needs. One night, as a teenager, I joined in a prayer circle with a large group of people who had gathered together to anoint with oil, lay hands on, and pray for a middle-aged man in our church who was dying of advanced-stage cancer. The diagnosis was not good and his doctors had given up hope that he would survive his fight. Yet a few months after we prayed our hearts out that night during the prayer meeting, his wife informed our church that her husband was cancer free! God had miraculously healed this man of terminal cancer. There was no other medical explanation for the miracle that had just happened in our church body.

I consider myself blessed to have known and experienced God's healing power from a very young age. These firsthand encounters with miraculous healings continued when our family served as cross-cultural missionaries in the country of Russia for twelve years. As a young married couple on the mission field, my wife, Cara, and I were not able to conceive a child for the first eight years of our marriage. Due to some physical challenges, we struggled to get pregnant and start a family. In 2006, when the very first TLC (Wellsprings of Freedom International) team came to serve in Russia, Cara and I were both ministered to in individual freedom sessions. Towards the end of her first session, the team gathered around Cara, laid hands on her, and prayed in faith for physical healing in the name of Jesus. She physically felt things moving inside her body as they prayed for Jesus to heal her closed womb. The very next day, she began her monthly cycle—something that hadn't happened for almost a year. A few months later, we were able to conceive a child, only to tragically lose him to a miscarriage at the end of the first trimester. As painful and heartbreaking as that experience was, we held onto hope that we could one day have children. Exactly one year later, by God's grace, Cara conceived again and gave birth to a healthy and beautiful baby girl, Sophia. She is truly our "miracle child"!

The miraculous healings continued throughout our years of missionary service. One Sunday evening, a middle-aged Russian woman visited our church for the very first time. While engaging her in conversation before the worship service, she was unable to make eye contact with me. I noticed that she seemed to be having a difficult time focusing her eyesight. In the middle of our conversation, she ashamedly apologized for her inability to look straight at me. She told me that the week before, her alcoholic husband had beaten her so badly that she temporarily lost eyesight in her right eye. My heart went out to this woman, and I quickly learned that this kind of verbal, emotional, and physical abuse had gone on in her home for years. She then informed me that the very same thing happened the year before. But that time, she temporarily lost her vision in her left eye. She was a broken woman and in desperate need of help.

Within a few weeks after attending our church, this precious Russian woman gave her life to Christ. Knowing her dire situation, I told her about our Wellsprings of Freedom ministry and how I believed it could help her find healing and freedom in Christ. After answering some of her initial questions, I invited her to sign up for her own freedom sessions with our ministry team. A few weeks later, she came in for her first session, and the Holy Spirit began to reveal all the wounded areas of her life that needed deep-level healing. As she worked through forgiveness of her abusive alcoholic husband, many deep wounds were healed, and the heavy demonic oppression was lifted off. Our team then gathered around and laid hands on her, and prayed for physical healing of her eyesight, in Jesus' name.

A week later, our client returned for her second session. When I asked her how she was feeling, she began to tell our team how transformational her first session was. She couldn't believe the difference. She felt so much better! When I asked about the eyesight in her right eye, she looked at me and paused for a moment. She then looked around the room at my team members, smiled, and said, "You know, I haven't even thought much about it over the last week, because it's so natural. But my vision is clear now! I can see clearly again!" God had miraculously healed and restored this woman's sight (Luke 4:18). As a result, her faith was strengthened and she quickly began to tell others about the healing power of Jesus.

Both on the mission field and upon returning to the United States, I have seen the constant physical needs that are all around us. Not a week goes by at Wellsprings of Freedom International (WFI) that we don't encounter a client who is suffering physically from chronic pain, fibromyalgia, arthritis, migraine headaches, back pain, severe allergies, sleep disorders, anxiety disorders, multiple sclerosis, or a serious form of cancer. The need for physical healing is everywhere. And the church of Jesus Christ has an incredible opportunity to reveal God's healing power to those who are sick, tormented, and afflicted. This is why in 2013, Wellsprings of Freedom International launched the physical healing prayer sessions that are now offered two to three times a week at our Healing Center in Rock Island, Illinois.

Over the years, we have observed many people in our community who are fearful or apprehensive about going through freedom sessions at WFI. They may have had negative experiences with a healing or deliverance ministry in the past. They may hold negative stereotypes of deliverance ministry in their minds from Hollywood movies and sensational TV shows. They may have been turned off by eccentric faith healers on Christian television. Or they may not feel like they are ready to deal with all the "garbage" in their past. But they are struggling physically and are genuinely seeking healing. It is this group of people who can now be reached and touched through the physical healing prayer sessions at WFI.

The physical healing prayer sessions are one-hour prayer sessions that focus predominantly on healing prayer for physical needs. Like the three-hour freedom sessions offered at WFI, the physical healing prayer sessions are also team-based (consisting of a Team Leader, at least two Discerners, and an Intercessor). While the training for team members on our physical healing prayer teams is the same for all WFI team members (as outlined in great detail in our first book, "With Gentle Authority"), the physical healing prayer sessions tend to take on a life of their own.

We recognize that there are many different methods and models of praying for the sick. We also acknowledge that the physical healing prayer sessions are not the only time when a follower of Jesus can pray for healing. Prayer for physical healing can happen during or after worship services, in large gatherings and healing prayer services, in homes or home groups, in public places outside the church walls, and when meeting one-on-one with a friend. This book, however, is our attempt to outline the unique Wellsprings of Freedom method of healing prayer that the Holy Spirit has revealed and taught us in recent years. It has proven to be a powerful and effective model of physical healing prayer. This method helps to provide an overarching uniformity to all of the physical healing prayer teams and sessions that are offered each week at WFI in Rock Island, Illinois. It is built upon sixteen years of collective experience in the WFI ministry and is done with the utmost love, compassion, gentleness, and respect for the client.

As a healing ministry, we humbly acknowledge that the power to heal comes not from us, but from God alone. Healing does not happen by our own might, human wisdom, power, or strength. Nor does it occur by our own striving or human effort. It is only by the power of God's Spirit working in and through us that the sick are healed and prisoners are set free (Zechariah 4:6). We are merely the vessels through which God's healing power flows. We are "fragile clay jars" to show that this all-surpassing power is from God and not from us (2 Corinthians 4:7). Jesus is the Vine, we are the branches. If He remains in us and we remain in Him, we will bear much fruit. Apart from Him we can do nothing (John 15:1-5).

I am so thankful to Lynette Johnson and her physical healing prayer teams who faithfully serve at Wellsprings of Freedom International each week. May this book be a blessing to all who read it and to all who desire to know and experience Jesus' power and authority to heal the sick, cast out demons, cure diseases, and preach the kingdom of God (Luke 9:1-2).

Chapter 1

God Still Heals Today

"Through the Wellsprings of Freedom ministry I have received healing from depression and healing from fear. I have a better relationship with Jesus now. When I first came to Wellsprings of Freedom, I was diagnosed with a cancerous tumor. The team that I was with prayed for healing and now the tumor is GONE! Jesus healed me!" (C.P.)

In 2014, a middle-aged woman came into my (Brian's) office and shared her story with tears of joy. She told me how one year earlier, she underwent a serious back operation to help alleviate severe pain in her lower back and legs. Then, just two weeks prior to our conversation, she re-injured her back, and once again, felt paralyzed with pain so severe she could hardly move.

Shortly before this woman entered my office, she had asked a physical healing prayer team at Wellsprings of Freedom International to pray for healing. As the team was worshipping, this woman already began to feel the physical pain leave her body. And when the team members gathered around her to pray over her in Jesus' name, they noticed that one of her legs was significantly longer than the other. While the team continued to pray for healing, they literally saw her legs begin to move and come back into alignment with each other. By the end of their prayer time, the woman's legs were evened out and her back pain was completely gone. She was miraculously healed in the name of Jesus!

This woman's story is a powerful testimony that *God still heals today*. When we read the Gospels, we notice how Jesus frequently healed the sick and gave sight to the blind. He made the mute speak and enabled the deaf to hear. He healed the lepers and raised the dead back to life. Physical healings were clear signs of God's kingdom coming to earth.

There are some who argue that God no longer heals today. They argue that miraculous healings were experienced by the Early Church in the first century in order to display God's mighty power and to help establish Christ's Church on earth. Once the Church was established, miraculous healings ceased to exist. This represents the historic Cessationist position, which claims that the spiritual gifts such as prophecy, tongues, and healing were confined to the first century and were used at the time the apostles were establishing the young churches and the New Testament was not yet complete.[1]

Yet Scripture, church history, reason, and experience all seem to paint a very different picture. They all seem to confirm the above testimony—that physical, emotional, and spiritual healings do still happen today all around the world. In fact, for many Christians living in the non-Western world, physical healings, miracles, signs and wonders are a normal part of everyday church life.

I often wonder how many more people could be healed if we would just step out in faith and boldly pray for them in Jesus' name. When we do not practice or encourage prayer for the sick, are we essentially limiting God's ability to heal? Perhaps our theology needs to be healed before our bodies can be healed? These are valid questions worth asking, and questions that I pray many Christians living in the Western world will seriously consider.

Our God Is Healer

In Old Testament times, names carried significant meaning. They did more than simply distinguish one person from another.

Names often conveyed a person's essential character or nature. This is especially true of the names of God revealed to us in the Bible.

In Exodus 15, God reveals Himself to the Israelites as Jehovah-Rapha, which in Hebrew means "The Lord Who Heals." "He said, 'If you will listen carefully to the voice of the Lord your God and do what is right in his sight, obeying his commands and keeping all his decrees, then I will not make you suffer any of the diseases that I sent on the Egyptians; *for I am the Lord who heals you*" (15:26, NLT). God's name revealed in this passage emphasizes His authority and power to heal (physically, spiritually, mentally, and emotionally). It communicates that healing is a part of God's nature and His mission on earth. God's heart longs to heal. Healing is His passion.

The Hebrew Scriptures point to God as the source of all healing.[2] We read in Psalm 147:3 that He is a God "who heals the brokenhearted and bandages their wounds" (NLT). In Psalm 103, King David offers up a song of praise to God for who He is—a God "who forgives all your sins and heals all your diseases" (103:3). David testifies in Psalm 41:3 that "The Lord sustains them on their sickbed and restores them from their bed of illness" (NIV). He is the Healer of all sickness and brokenness. In Jeremiah 31, the prophet declares God's promise of hope, healing, and restoration to the Israelites by saying; "'But I will restore you to health and heal your wounds,' declares the Lord" (31:17).

Isaiah 35 gives us a glimpse of the coming messianic kingdom, when God himself would rule and reign, and evil and death and sickness would finally be defeated. Healing would characterize His kingdom and God's *shalom* (wholeness) would be restored on earth.[3] Isaiah writes:

"Strengthen the feeble hands, steady the knees that give way; say to those with fearful hearts, 'Be strong, do not fear; your God will come, he will come with vengeance; with divine retribution he will come to save you.' *Then the eyes of the blind will be opened and the ears of the deaf unstopped. Then will the lame leap like a deer, and the mute tongue shout for joy.* Water will gush forth in the wilderness and streams in the desert" (35:3-6, NIV).

Later, in Isaiah 53, the prophet looks ahead to the time of the "Suffering Servant"—the coming Messiah—who would take the sin and evil of the world upon Himself. He would be "despised and rejected by men, a man of sorrows, and familiar with suffering" (Isaiah 53:3). There would be nothing beautiful or majestic about His appearance (53:2). Instead of riding victoriously into Jerusalem as the long-awaited conquering King, He would humbly enter the city unarmed, riding on a donkey, and would eventually be put to death on a cross. Isaiah prophesies:

"Surely he took up our pain and bore our suffering, yet we considered him punished by God, stricken by him, and afflicted.[5] But he was pierced for our transgressions, he was crushed for our iniquities; the punishment that brought us peace was on him, *and by his wounds we are healed.*[6] We all, like sheep, have gone astray, each of us has turned to our own way; and the LORD has laid on him the iniquity of us all" (Isaiah 53:4-6, NIV).

Despite our rebellion—our fallen, sinful human condition—God had an answer for lost humanity. It was to send a Rescuer, One who could restore what was lost through the Fall. God Himself entered into our brokenness in order to make us whole. He took on human flesh and became like one of us so that we could be healed (John 1:14). In the greatest act of love the world has ever seen, the Creator entered into His creation to restore our lost inheritance. The injuries He suffered became our healing (Isaiah 53:5b, The Voice).

We see the clear fulfillment of this (Isaiah 53) prophecy in Matthew 8, where Matthew confirms that physical healing is an integral part of the redemptive mission of Christ on earth:

"When Jesus came into Peter's house, he saw Peter's mother-in-law lying in bed with a fever.[15] He touched her hand and the fever left her, and she got up and began to wait on him.[16] When evening came, many who were demon-possessed were brought to him, and he drove out the spirits with a word and healed all the sick.[17] This was to fulfill what was spoken through the prophet Isaiah: 'He took up our infirmities and bore our diseases.'" (Matthew 8:14-17, NIV)

why is this not happening today - why do they linger?

Jesus Christ Came to Heal

In the Gospels, God's nature is fully revealed to us in the person of Jesus Christ, who came to heal and to set the captives free. While in a synagogue in Nazareth, Jesus stands up and proclaims that the words of Isaiah 61:1-3 are being fulfilled in His coming to earth:

"The Spirit of the Lord is on me, because he has anointed me to preach good news to the poor. He has sent me to proclaim freedom for the prisoners and recovery of sight for the blind, to release the oppressed, to proclaim the year of the Lord's favor" (Luke 4:18-19).

Jesus rolled up the scroll from which He was reading, gave it back to the attendant, and sat down. The eyes of everyone in the synagogue were fastened on Him. And He announced to them, "Today this scripture is fulfilled in your hearing" (4:20-21).

Jesus publicly announces His kingdom mission and reveals the heart of God to heal. Salvation, healing, deliverance, and freedom are all made possible through Jesus Christ. He came to bring healing and deliverance to every aspect of our being—physical, emotional, and spiritual—through the power of the Holy Spirit.[4] He came to break the power of Satan (1 John 3:8) and the curse of sin, death, sickness, and disease (Galatians 3:13-14). From this point forward, the Gospel of Luke tells of how Jesus went from village to village healing the sick, casting out demons, and preaching the kingdom of God. The people brought to Jesus all who had various kinds of sicknesses and diseases, and laying His hands on each one, He healed them (Luke 4:40-41).

In his seminal work, *The Gospel of the Kingdom*, George Elton Ladd explains, "Our Lord's ministry and announcement of the Good News of the Kingdom were characterized by healing, and most notably by the casting out of demons. He proclaimed the Good News of the Kingdom of God, and He demonstrated the Good News of the Kingdom of God by delivering men from the bondage of Satan."[5]

In the very next chapter, Luke 5, we read the story of how Jesus miraculously heals a man covered with leprosy (5:12-14). News about Jesus spread more and more, so that crowds of people came to hear Him and to be healed of their sicknesses (5:15). Immediately following this astonishing display of God's power, Jesus then heals a paralytic who was lowered down through the roof of the house on his mat:

"One day as he was teaching, Pharisees and teachers of the law, who had come from every village of Galilee and from Judea and Jerusalem, were sitting there. *And the power of the Lord was present for him to heal the sick.*[18] Some men came carrying a paralyzed man on a mat and tried to take him into the house to lay him before Jesus.[19] When they could not find a way to do this because of the crowd, they went up on the roof and lowered him on his mat through the tiles into the middle of the crowd, right in front of Jesus.[20] When Jesus saw their faith, he said, 'Friend, your sins are forgiven.'[21] The Pharisees and the teachers of the law began thinking to themselves, 'Who is this fellow who speaks blasphemy? Who can forgive sins but God alone?'[22] Jesus knew what they were thinking and asked, 'Why are you thinking these things in your hearts?[23] Which is easier: to say, "Your sins are forgiven," or to say, "Get up and walk"?[24] But I want you to know that the Son of Man has authority on earth to forgive sins.' So he said to the paralyzed man, 'I tell you, get up, take your mat and go home.'[25] Immediately he stood up in front of them, took what he had been lying on and went home praising God.[26] Everyone was amazed and gave praise to God. They were filled with awe and said, '"We have seen remarkable things today"' (Luke 5:17-26, NIV).

In Matthew 4:23-25, at the beginning of Jesus' earthly ministry shortly after He began calling His first disciples to follow Him, Matthew writes:

"Jesus traveled throughout the region of Galilee, teaching in the synagogues and announcing the Good News about the Kingdom. *And he healed every kind of disease and illness.*[24] News about him spread as far as Syria, and people soon began bringing to him all who were sick. And whatever their sickness or disease, or if they were demon possessed or epileptic or paralyzed—*he healed them all.*[25] Large crowds followed him wherever he went—people from Galilee, the Ten Towns, Jerusalem, from all over Judea, and from east of the Jordan River" (NLT).

New Testament scholars believe that this region of Galilee where Jesus travelled and ministered in the first century had a population of around three hundred thousand people living in two hundred or more villages and towns.[6] In this area, large crowds would often follow Jesus. People came in a hurry when they heard about the miraculous healings that Jesus was performing. They had never seen anything like it. Truly, Jesus was the Son of God, the Lord's Anointed, the Messiah. Ironically, in many of these instances in the Gospels, the simple and the poor followed Jesus in crowds because they saw what was happening in their midst, while the Jewish religious leaders were threatened, questioned Jesus' authority, and tried to figure it all out.[7]

In Matthew 9:18-34, Jesus performs a series of three miracles that demonstrate His deep compassion for those who were sick, suffering, and on the margins of society. Beginning in verse 18, a synagogue leader ("ruler") came and knelt before Jesus in desperation. He cried out and said, "My daughter has just died. But come and put your hand on her, and she will live." So Jesus got up and went with him, along with His disciples.

While they were on their way, a woman who had suffered for twelve years from constant bleeding came up behind Jesus (9:20). The Gospel of Mark mentions that this woman had suffered a great deal under the care of many doctors and had spent all she had. Yet instead of getting better, her condition grew worse (Mark 5:25-26). In desperation, she reached out and touched the edge of His robe, for she thought to herself, "If I can just touch his robe, I will be healed" (Matthew 9:21). Jesus turned around, saw her, and said to her, "Take heart, daughter… your faith has healed you." The woman who had suffered terribly from twelve years of hemorrhaging was miraculously healed at that moment (9:22). Her childlike faith in Christ's healing power had healed her.

Afterwards, Jesus arrived at the synagogue ruler's home (9:23). Upon seeing the crowd, the flute players, and all the commotion, he sent them all out of the room where the daughter's body was lying. Jesus then went in, took the dead girl by the hand, and she stood up! Jesus brought the dead back to life, demonstrating His power over death. News about this miracle spread rapidly throughout the entire region (9:25-26).

As Jesus went on from there, two blind men followed him and shouted, "Son of David, have mercy on us!" (9:27). They went right into the house where Jesus was staying, and He asked them, "Do you believe I can make you see?" "Yes, Lord," they replied, "We do" (9:28). Jesus physically touched their eyes and said, "Because of your faith, it will happen" (9:29). Then their eyes were opened and their sight was restored. News about Jesus continued to spread all over that area (9:30-31).

One of the most powerful testimonies about Jesus is found in Matthew 11:1-6. When John the Baptist heard about all the miracles Christ was doing, he sent his disciples to ask Him, "Are you the Messiah we've been expecting, or should we keep looking for someone else?" In response to their question, Jesus replied, "Go back to John and tell him what you have heard and seen— *the blind see, the lame walk, the lepers are cured, the deaf hear, the dead are raised to life, and the Good News is being preached to the poor*" (11:4-5, NLT). Jesus was demonstrating that He was the long-awaited Messiah, precisely because He healed the sick, raised the dead, and restored sight to the blind. The damage done by the Fall (Genesis 3) was now being undone. God had come to help His people (Luke 7:16)! Death and evil were being defeated. The future age was invading this present evil age. God's new world was breaking in to establish His rule and reign on the earth.

Commissioned to Heal

Jesus not only proclaimed and demonstrated the power of the kingdom. He also imparted that same power and authority to His disciples. In Matthew 10, when Jesus called His twelve disciples together, He gave them power and authority to drive out evil spirits and to heal every kind of sickness and disease (10:1). His kingdom message was to be their message:

"Go and announce to them that the Kingdom of Heaven is near. Heal the sick, raise the dead, cure those with leprosy, and cast out demons. Give as freely as you have received!" (Matthew 10:7-8, NLT)

Jesus commissioned and bestowed His authority on His disciples to do the works of the Father. In John 14:12, He told His disciples, "I tell you the truth, anyone who has faith in me will do what I have been doing. He will do even greater things than these, because I am going to the Father" (NIV). Jesus healed the sick, cured diseases, and cast out demons. And then He promised that His disciples would do even greater works than these! They were to live as Jesus lived—to be His hands and feet to the world. They were to carry on His powerful kingdom ministry.

The Gospel of Mark tells us that as the twelve were sent out, they went and preached that people everywhere should repent of their sins and turn to God. They drove out many demons and anointed many sick people with oil and healed them (6:6-13).

At the end of Mark's Gospel, Jesus commissions His disciples to "go into all the world and preach the Good News to everyone" (16:15). He promised that these miraculous signs would accompany those who believe: "They will cast out demons in my name, and they will speak in new languages. They will be able to handle snakes with safety, and if they drink anything poisonous, it won't hurt them. They will be able to place their hands on the sick, and they will be healed" (16:17-18, NLT).

After sending out the twelve (Luke 9:1-6, Matthew 10), Jesus later chose and sent out seventy-two other disciples in pairs ahead of Him, to all the towns and places He planned to visit (Luke 10:1). They also were commissioned to do the works of the kingdom:

"If you enter a town and it welcomes you, eat whatever is set before you. Heal the sick, and tell them, 'the Kingdom of God is near you now'" (10:8-9, NLT).

Before His ascension into heaven, Jesus commanded His disciples not to leave Jerusalem, but to wait for the gift His Father had promised (Acts 1:4). For John had baptized with water, but in a few days, they would be baptized with the Holy Spirit (1:5). He explained; "…You will receive power when the Holy Spirit comes on you; and you will be my witnesses in Jerusalem, and in all Judea and Samaria, and to the ends of the earth" (1:8). If we truly are Christ's disciples, then we also have been commissioned and empowered by the Holy Spirit to be His witnesses, to pray for the sick, to preach the kingdom of God, and to cast out demons.

Healing in the Early Church

Following Christ's ascension (Luke 24:50-53, Acts 1:9-11), the New Testament Church continued to pray for healings, miracles, signs and wonders. Shortly after the Day of Pentecost, when Peter and John were going up to the temple to pray, Peter miraculously heals a man who was crippled from birth (Acts 3:1-10). All the people were astonished and came running towards Peter and John in the place called Solomon's Colonnade. When Peter saw this, he said to the crowd, "By faith in the name of Jesus, this man whom you see and know was made strong. It is Jesus' name and the faith that comes through him that has given this complete healing to him, as you can all see" (3:16, NIV).

In Acts 4, when the believers raised their voices together in prayer, they asked the Lord to "Stretch out your hand to heal and perform miraculous signs and wonders through the name of your holy servant Jesus" (4:30). One chapter later, Luke tells us how the apostles performed many miraculous signs and wonders among the people (5:12). More and more people believed on the Lord Jesus Christ, and as a result, people brought the sick into the streets and laid them on mats so that Peter's shadow might fall on some of them as he passed by. Crowds also gathered from the towns around Jerusalem, bringing their sick and those tormented by evil spirits, *and all of them were healed* (5:14-16).

After a great persecution broke out against the church in Jerusalem after the death of Stephen, all the believers except the apostles were scattered throughout Judea and Samaria (Acts 8:1). Luke records that Philip went down to a city in Samaria and told the people there about Jesus the Messiah (8:4-5). When the crowds of people heard Philip's message and saw the miraculous signs he performed, they all paid close attention to what he said. With shrieks, evil spirits came out of many people, and many who had been paralyzed or crippled were healed. So there was great joy in that city (8:6-8).

In Acts 10, the apostle Peter explains to Cornelius' household, "And you know that God anointed Jesus of Nazareth with the Holy Spirit and with power. Then Jesus went around doing good and healing all who were oppressed by the devil, for God was with him" (10:38). On Paul's missionary journeys, we read incredible stories of how people were miraculously healed. While in the city of Ephesus, God did such extraordinary miracles through Paul so that even handkerchiefs and aprons that had touched him were taken to the sick and they were healed of their illnesses and delivered from evil spirits (Acts 19:11-12)!

Finally, in James 5, the apostle James encourages believers who were scattered throughout the Roman Empire in the first century to call on the elders of the church if they are sick, so they might pray over them and anoint the sick with oil. James teaches that "...the prayer offered in faith will make the sick person well; the Lord will raise him up. If he has sinned, he will be forgiven. Therefore, confess your sins to each other and pray for each other so that you may be healed. The prayer of a righteous person is powerful and effective" (5:13-16).

From beginning to end, the Bible is filled with promises and stories of healing. It reveals a God who heals, who is called the Great Physician. It teaches us that healing is a part of *who God is* and *what He does*. Healing is a part of God's coming kingdom to earth.

Scripture offers us hope that there is no sickness that can't be healed. There is no disease so far advanced that can't be cured. There is no condition that can't be reversed. Jesus Christ is the same yesterday, today, and forever (Hebrews 13:8). He healed in New Testament times and still miraculously heals today. He does not change like the shifting shadows (James 1:17). He is the Creator and author of life. He is the One who formed us with His own hands and knit us together in our mother's womb (Psalm 139). He knows all about our needs and has complete power and authority to heal us.

Endnotes

1 Stanley N. Gundry & Wayne A. Grudem. *Are Miraculous Gifts For Today? Four Views* (Grand Rapids, MI: Zondervan , 2011). Location 55.

2 Ann Spangler. *The Names of God* (Grand Rapids, MI: Zondervan, 2009), p. 42.

3 Alexander F. Venter. *Doing Healing: How to Minister God's Healing in the Power of the Spirit* (Cape Town, South Africa: Vineyard International Publishing, 2009), p. 76.

4 Francis MacNutt. *The Healing Reawakening: Reclaiming Our Lost Inheritance* (Grand Rapids, MI: Chosen Books, 2005), p. 11.

5 George Elton Ladd. *The Gospel of the Kingdom: Scriptural Studies in the Kingdom of God* (Grand Rapids, MI: Eerdmans Publishing, 1959), p. 47.

6 Wilkins, Michael J. NIV *Application Commentary, New Testament: Matthew* (Grand Rapids, MI: Zondervan: Grand Rapids, MI, 2004), p. 180.

7 Francis MacNutt. *Healing (Revised and Expanded)* (Notre Dame, IN: Ave Maria Press, 1999), p. 18.

Chapter 2

Sickness and Demonization

"For six years, I lived my life in sadness and constant pain. I had so many medical issues: several surgeries to remove three tumors from various parts of my body, joint, back, and neck pain, migraine headaches, and fibromyalgia. I was miserable. Sometimes I cried in pain just to put my clothes on. I was using codeine, Vicodin, and other medications on a daily basis just to tolerate the pain.

"In 2015, I agreed to have a session with a mission team from Wellsprings of Freedom International that was serving at my church. Throughout the session, the team led me through a healing process of some of my deepest wounds. I felt God's presence and His great love for me. And with the help of a dedicated team, I was SET FREE of so much anger, unforgiveness, and lies of a fortune-teller that I had believed for almost thirty years. Years of demonic oppression was broken off in the name of Jesus. I could finally move my fingers for the first time without any pain! My legs, joints, and skin were free of pain! I cried—no longer out of pain, but out of joy! Though I was advised by the team not to stop my medications and to follow-up with my doctor, I went home and said, 'Lord, You healed me! I don't feel any pain!' So I threw my meds away. God's grace was upon me because I had absolutely no withdrawal symptoms at all!

"I thank God for Wellsprings of Freedom—for their love and for their obedience to Him to set this captive FREE! To Him be all the glory!" (C.M.)

As we study the life and ministry of Jesus, we notice how He frequently encountered men and women who were sick, demonized, and suffering physically. Throughout the Gospels, Jesus is seen healing the sick and casting out demons in the same passages (see Matthew 4:23-25, 16-17, 10:1, Mark 1:32-34, Luke 4:40-41). Physical healing and deliverance were very much interconnected when Jesus taught, preached the kingdom of God, physically touched, and prayed with people. He not only healed those whose spirits were sick and in need of deliverance or forgiveness; he also healed those whose bodies were sick, lame, blind, and leprous.[1]

What is the relationship between sickness and demonization? Is all sickness caused by demons? Can some sicknesses and diseases be caused by Satan? Or is sickness the result of sin in our lives? Do some sicknesses and diseases have a natural cause, merely the result of living in a fallen, broken world? How did Jesus view and interact with sickness and disease?

As written in the powerful personal testimony mentioned above, sixteen years of experience in the Wellsprings of Freedom ministry has taught us that human beings, including believers in Jesus Christ, can be physically afflicted by evil spirits (demonized). While there are certainly natural causes to sickness and disease, Scripture confirms that there can also be demonic causes to physical and mental illness. Below are four examples from the Gospels that illustrate this spiritual reality.

A Crippled Woman

In Luke 13:10-17, while teaching in a synagogue, Jesus encounters a woman who had been *crippled by an evil spirit for eighteen years*. She was bent over and was not able to stand up straight. Luke writes:

"On a Sabbath Jesus was teaching in one of the synagogues,[11] and a woman was there who had been crippled by a spirit for eighteen years. She was bent over and could not straighten up at all.[12] When Jesus saw her, he called her forward and said to her, 'Woman, you are set free from your infirmity.'[13] Then he put his hands on her, and immediately she straightened up and praised God.[14] Indignant because Jesus had healed on the Sabbath, the synagogue leader said to the people, 'There are six days for work. So come and be healed on those days, not on the Sabbath.'[15] The Lord answered him, 'You hypocrites! Doesn't each of you on the Sabbath untie your ox or donkey from the stall and lead it out to give it water?[16] Then should not this woman, a daughter of Abraham, whom Satan has kept bound for eighteen long years, be set free on the Sabbath day from what bound her?'[17] When he said this, all his opponents were humiliated, but the people were delighted with all the wonderful things he was doing." (NIV)

It is evident from the story that the presence of an evil spirit was causing her body to be physically weak and bent over. The fact that this woman had been suffering for eighteen years emphasizes the seriousness of her physical condition. Even Luke, a trained medical doctor, acknowledges that the source of this woman's suffering is spiritual. There is no other diagnosis given for her condition. Some New Testament scholars claim that her situation involved either some type of bone degeneration or muscular paralysis.[2] Whatever the actual physical condition may have been, Jesus seems to refer to it as a spirit of infirmity afflicting her body. He called the woman forward and said, "Woman, you are set free from your infirmity" (10:12). He then touched her and instantly she could stand up straight and praised God!

When opposition arose from the synagogue ruler because Jesus healed this woman on the Sabbath, He exposed their hypocrisy and lack of compassion for broken and hurting people. Jesus openly acknowledges that this woman was a "daughter of Abraham" (a Jewish believer), whose body was bound by *Satan* for eighteen long years. Clearly, Jesus discerns that the source of this woman's physical suffering was demonic in nature. He has eyes to see that this woman was a victim of Satan's evil forces. And out of deep compassion, He longed to heal her of her infirmity.

This story illustrates that although Satan may cause sickness, Jesus Christ has full power and authority to heal sickness. There is nothing that Satan has done that Christ cannot undo. This includes healing physical deformities, sickness, and disease.

A Young Demonized Boy

In Mark 9, while Peter, James, and John were witnessing Jesus' transfiguration before their very eyes up on a high mountain, a desperate father brought his demonized son to Jesus' other disciples for help. An argument ensued among them, and when Jesus returned, He saw the large crowd that had gathered. "What is all this arguing about?" Jesus asked (9:16, NLT). The father cried out, "Teacher, I brought you my son, who is possessed by a spirit that has robbed him of speech. Whenever it seizes him, it throws him to the ground. He foams at the mouth, gnashes his teeth and becomes rigid. I asked your disciples to drive out the spirit, but they could not" (9:17-18, NIV).

When Jesus asked the father to bring the boy to Him, the evil spirit threw the child into a violent convulsion and he fell to the ground. He rolled around, writhing and foaming at the mouth (9:19-20). Jesus learned from the father that his son had been in this condition since childhood. The evil spirit had often thrown him into fire or water to kill him (9:21-22). Jesus had mercy on this young boy, and when he saw that a crowd of onlookers was running to the scene, he rebuked the evil spirit. *"You deaf and mute spirit,"* he said, "I command you, come out of him and never enter him again" (9:25). Immediately, the spirit shrieked, convulsed the boy violently, and left him (9:26). Jesus then took him by the hand, helped him to his feet, and he stood up (9:27). The boy was delivered and healed of a demonic spirit that had tormented him physically, mentally, and emotionally for years. Now he was finally free!

Afterward, when Jesus was alone in the house with his disciples, they asked Him privately: "Why couldn't we cast out the evil spirit?" (9:28, NLT). After all, Jesus had given them authority over evil spirits and they had experienced success (see Mark 3:13-19, 6:6b-13). But this particular case was problematic for them. Jesus explained that this kind can be cast out only "by prayer" (9:29). Apparently, His disciples were too busy arguing with the teachers of the law to take time to pray.

In this account, we see that demons do have the ability to harass, afflict, and torment human beings physically (as well as mentally, emotionally, and spiritually)—including young children. They have the power to physically manifest in and through our bodies at times, causing intense pain and suffering (i.e. seizures, convulsions, shaking, tremors, trembling, migraine headaches, etc.). Demons not only can influence the behavior of human beings, but can also influence our bodies and health. Interestingly, in this instance, Jesus both discerned and called out the demon that was afflicting the boy by name—a "deaf and mute spirit."

A Blind and Mute Man

Matthew 12 describes another instance of a demonized man who was both blind and mute (12:22). Once again, it is clear from Matthew's account that this man's blindness and inability to speak was a result of the activity of unclean spirits. This man was brought to Jesus and was miraculously healed, so that he could both talk and see. His deliverance led to physical healing and full restoration of his hearing and eyesight. All the people were astonished and asked, "Could it be that Jesus is the Son of David, the Messiah?" (12:23, NLT).

Jesus' power and authority amazed the crowds, but stunned the Pharisees. He commanded the demons to leave by His own authority, and they left! The Pharisees, however, accused Jesus of using the power of Beelzebub (the prince of demons) to cast out demons (12:24). Knowing their hearts and seeing the flaws in their arguments, Jesus exposed their spiritual blindness. He pointed out that:

"Every kingdom divided against itself will be ruined, and every city or household divided against itself will not stand. If Satan drives out Satan, he is divided against himself. How then can his kingdom stand? And if I drive out demons by Beelzebub, by whom do your people drive them out? So then, they will be your judges. But if I drive out demons by the Spirit of God, then the kingdom of God has come upon you" (Matthew 12:25-28, NIV).

Simon Peter's Mother-in-Law and Crowds of Sick People

In Luke 4:38-39, Jesus left the synagogue in the town of Capernaum, where He had just healed a demonized man (4:31-37), and went to the home of Simon Peter. Luke records that Simon's mother-in-law was very sick with a high fever. Those who were present in the home pleaded with Jesus to help her. "'Please heal her,' everyone begged" (4:38b, NLT). Standing at her bedside, Jesus bent over her and rebuked the fever, and it left her. We are told that she got up at once and prepared a meal for them (4:39)! Just as Jesus had delivered the man from an evil spirit in the synagogue, so He now heals Simon's mother-in-law of sickness.

Those of us who have grown up and live in Western cultures or have been educated in the West (which espouses a naturalistic, materialistic, and scientific worldview), tend to have a difficult time grasping the concept that Jesus actually *rebuked* the fever in Simon's mother-in-law's body. The idea of speaking to non-personalities (to sickness, in this case) is completely foreign to the modern Western mind. This practice may even seem scandalous or too "charismatic" to many Western evangelical Christians. Yet Jesus, the perfect and sinless Son of God, clearly rebukes the fever, and it immediately leaves her body. (At other times, such as in Mark 11:12-14, 20-25, Jesus spoke directly to a fig tree and cursed it to teach His disciples a powerful lesson in faith.) This story testifies of Christ's power and authority over sickness and disease.

Afterward, when the sun was setting, Luke tells us that the people brought to Jesus all who had various kinds of sickness, and laying His hands on each one, He healed them. Moreover, demons came out of many people and shouted, "You are the Son of God!" But Jesus rebuked the evil spirits and would not allow them to speak, because they knew He was the Messiah (Luke 4:40-41). Once again, Jesus is healing the sick and casting out demons in the same passage. Why? Because the two are often linked together in Christ's kingdom ministry. When people are delivered from evil spirits, physical healing is often (but not always) the end result. We see this same pattern occurring in the Wellsprings of Freedom ministry today on a weekly basis.

Author Ken Blue comments that "the concrete reality of the coming of the Kingdom was evidenced in the defeat and driving off of sickness. It is all but impossible for modern Western people to see sickness the way Jesus understood it. For him, sickness was not explained in terms of germs or biological malfunctions, but in terms of personalized evil. Jesus saw Satan as the cause of all kinds of physical suffering."[3] He viewed sickness as an enemy to be defeated. He saw those who were sick as victims of unseen forces who needed to be healed and restored. His understanding of sickness and disease directly challenges our modern Western presuppositions and worldview. Yet even today, when praying for the sick in our ministry, we often uncover the presence of evil spirits which are connected to the physical symptoms of illness.

Not All Sickness Is Caused by Demonization

From these four Gospel accounts, we learn that it is certainly possible for evil spirits to attack our physical bodies and cause physical pain, suffering, sickness, and disease. At the same time, there is no indication in Scripture that *all* sickness and disease is caused by Satan and evil spirits either. Therefore, to answer the burning question, "Is all sickness caused by demons?", our answer would be no, but *some* sickness can be caused by Satan and his demonic forces. Those individuals who have been given the gift of discerning spirits (mentioned in 1 Corinthians 12:10), will be able to help the Team Leader and client determine whether or not there is a spiritual (demonic) cause to a client's physical condition during a physical healing prayer session.

Not All Sickness Is Caused by Sin

It is important to realize that not everyone Jesus miraculously healed of sickness or blindness was demonized. Nor was sin always the cause of their physical condition. For instance, in John 9, when Jesus encountered a man who was born blind, His disciples immediately attributed sin as the cause of this man's blindness: "Rabbi, who sinned, this man or his parents, that he was born blind?" (9:2). They assumed that there was a connection between sin and this man's suffering (blindness). This line of thinking was part of the prevailing Jewish worldview of the day. Yet Jesus challenged their widely-held assumptions. He knew that His disciples were too quick to place blame on the source of this man's blindness. Their thinking was too naïve and simplistic to understand the complexities of physical suffering. He responded by explaining, "Neither this man nor his parents sinned…but this happened so that the work of God might be displayed in his life" (9:3). Or as the New Living Translation states, "This happened so the power of God could be seen in him."

The challenge with this passage is that it is often misunderstood by Christians. Jesus is not saying here that God caused the blindness or made this man blind so that He could reveal His power. God is not a cruel Father who would cause His children to suffer in this manner. He is a good Father, who delights to show mercy to His children. This common misunderstanding is largely due to the fact that the verse is not completely translated accurately from the New Testament Greek into most modern English language versions of the Bible. The text in verse 3 literally reads: "'Neither this man or his parents sinned,' said Jesus. 'But so that the work of God might be displayed in his life, we must do the work of him who sent me while it is still day'" (9:3).[4] Jesus understood that it did the blind man no good to know who sinned or what caused his physical suffering. Instead, He saw the blindness as a divine opportunity to bring healing and wholeness to a broken individual.

This narrative in John 9 illustrates how we as Christians must exercise caution about attributing *all* forms of sickness and disease to sin or demonization. In Jesus' encounters with sick people, He seemed to demonstrate the ability to discern the difference between sickness caused by natural means and sickness that was of satanic origin.[5] Given the multiple causes of sickness and disease attested to by Scripture, it takes spiritual discernment to know what is the cause in any given situation, what is the proper avenue of cure, and whether God wishes to heal at the spiritual, emotional, and/or physical levels, completely in the here and now, or whether He wishes to heal completely at the resurrection.[6]

The Early Church Fathers

When one moves beyond the time of the New Testament and looks across the history of the first four centuries of the Early Church, there are numerous written accounts of divine healings and exorcisms. It appears that stories of miraculous physical healings were quite frequent from this historical time period. Following the ministry model of Jesus and the apostles, prayer for deliverance from evil spirits often resulted in physical healing.

During the first hundred years of the Early Church, which is often referred to as "The Apostolic Age," healing and deliverance was a common practice and experience in Christian life.

In fact, physical healings (and other miraculous phenomena) help to explain the remarkable growth of Christianity during this period.[7] Yale historian Ramsay MacMullen researched and claims that in the next generation (after Christ), the apostles' success in winning recruits arose primarily from their miraculous deeds; above all, in healing.[8]

Irenaeus (c. 125-202 A.D.), an Early Church father and apologist, in his *Against Heresies: Book 1*, observes the following about the life and ministry of the Early Church in the second century:

"For some do certainly and truly drive out devils, so that those who have thus been cleansed from evil spirits frequently both believe (in Christ) and join themselves to the Church. Others have foreknowledge of things to come: they see visions, and utter prophetic expressions. Others still heal the sick by laying their hands upon them, and they are made whole. Yea, moreover, as I have said, the dead even have been raised up and remained among us for many years. And what shall I more say? It is not possible to name the number of gifts which the Church, (scattered) throughout the world, has received from God, in the name of Jesus Christ, who was crucified under Pontus Pilate, and which she exerts day by day for the benefit of the Gentiles, neither practicing deception upon any, nor taking any reward from them (on account of such miraculous interpositions). For as she has received freely from God, freely does she also minister (to others.)"[9]

Historical records from *every* century of the Christian Church contain similar reports and seem to confirm that divine healing was normative in the life of the Early Church. Just like in the New Testament, physical healing was often accompanied with deliverance from demonic spirits. Demonization was clearly viewed as a valid source of sickness and disease. As another well-known Church father, Tertullian (c. 155–220 A.D.), once observed, "How many men of rank (to say nothing of common people) have been delivered from devils, and healed of diseases!"[10]

Although the number of miraculous healings and exorcisms that were recorded throughout the Middle Ages up until the Reformation seemed to decline, one can still find written testimonies of the sick being healed and delivered in Jesus' name. In the twentieth century, with the rise of Pentecostalism and Charismatic expressions of Christianity throughout the world, there was a marked increase in the number of miraculous healings that were once again being reported. This significant upswing in healings, exorcisms, miracles, signs and wonders, continues into the twenty-first century today.

Endnotes

1 Francis MacNutt. *Healing (Revised & Expanded)* (Notre Dame, IN: Ave Maria Press, 1999),. p. 50.

2 Bock, Darrell L. NIV *Application Commentary, New Testament: Luke* (Grand Rapids, MI: Zondervan, 1996), p. 373.

3 Ken Blue. *Authority To Heal* (Downers Grove, IL: InterVarsity Press, 1987), Location 722.

4 Burge, Gary M. NIV *Application Commentary, New Testament: John* (Grand Rapids, MI: Zondervan, 2000), p. 272.

5 Nystrom, David P. NIV *Application Commentary, New Testament: James* (Grand Rapids, MI: Zondervan, 1997), p. 306

6 Charles H. Talbert. *Reading Luke: A Literary and Theological Commentary on the Third Gospel* (Macon, GA: Smyth & Helwys Publishing, 2013), Location 2298.

7 John Wimber & Kevin Springer. *Power Healing* (New York: HarperOne, 1987), p. 41.

8 Ramsay MacMullen. *Christianizing the Roman Empire (A.D. 100-400)* (New Haven, CN: Yale University Press, 1984), p. 22.

9 Quoted in Wimber, *Power Healing*, pp. 41-42.

10 Tertullian. *Ad Scapulum (To Scapula): Chapter 4.* http://www.early-christianwritings.com/text/tertullian05.html

Chapter 3

Team Dynamics and Spiritual Gifts

The Wellsprings of Freedom International ministry is a team-based ministry, consisting of a minimum of four people on every Wellsprings team. Each team member must demonstrate a high level of spiritual maturity, strong Christian character, the gift of faith or healing (described later in this chapter), a wholehearted love for God and for those who are sick, deep compassion for the hurting and those suffering physically, and a firm commitment to confidentiality. They understand that *love* is the motivation for healing ministry.

As the ministry has developed over the years, three distinct roles have emerged on a WFI team, including on the physical healing prayer teams. These roles include a *Team Leader, Discerner(s),* and an *Intercessor.* Each role plays a vital part in the deliverance and healing process. No one role is more important than another, since all three roles are essential and all work together under the guidance and direction of the Holy Spirit to minister healing to an individual with physical needs. A core WFI team consists of a minimum of four people. Some Wellsprings teams may have several people functioning as Discerners (at least two) or Intercessors (one or two), but there should only be one designated Team Leader per team.

The Team Leader

The Team Leader carries the bulk of the decision-making responsibility in a physical healing prayer session. They function like a traffic cop, an orchestra conductor, or the director of a play. They are the "team captain," and nothing happens in a physical healing prayer session without the Team Leader's permission.

Preferably, Team Leaders are individuals who have been given spiritual gifts of leadership, wisdom, faith, healing, words of knowledge, and/or intercession. Under the leadership of the Holy Spirit, the Team Leader completely controls the flow and sets the spiritual tone of the session. They do the majority of the speaking and are the one who facilitates the entire prayer time.

A Team Leader is responsible for:

1. Welcoming the client and the opening introductions.
2. Answering any questions that a client may have.
3. Choosing the worship music that will be played in the session.
4. Praying for the session, praying protection over the client and team, and establishing firm boundaries around the physical healing prayer session, in Jesus' name.
5. Walking the client through all the steps of deliverance, inner healing, and healing prayer.
6. Sharing the majority of the biblical advice given to a client, including replacing the lies of demons with the truth from God's Word.

The Team Leader must remain calm, poised, and in control at all times, even if the session becomes difficult or when demons sometimes do unusual things to the client or team members. The Team Leader must not show fear or be intimidated, threatened, or offended by crude things occasionally spoken to them by evil spirits. If threats are made toward the client or a team member, it is the Team Leader's job to confront the demonic spirit(s), firmly rebuke the spirit(s) for making a threat, and remind them that they are subject to the authority of the Lord Jesus Christ.

If demons continue to resist, try to manifest in and through the body of the client or another team member during the session, or stubbornly refuse to leave, the Team Leader should not panic or become frustrated. Instead, they should remain firm and resolute, continue to pray, and use their greatest weapon in battle: God's Word. They are encouraged to quote key scriptures that confirm the power and authority of Christ (such as Luke 10:18-19, Colossians 2:9-10, 14-15, and 1 Peter 3:22). If and when a spirit is especially stubborn, resistant, prideful, or mouthy, the Team Leader should ask for mighty warrior angels to come and bind them up and usher them before Jesus. As they stand before Jesus, the demons should be forbidden (in Jesus' name) from turning their heads to the right or to the left, and should be commanded to look directly into the face of Jesus. Once their eyelids are forced open and they look at Jesus, they become far more compliant and cooperative. If necessary, demons may also need to be commanded and forbidden from cursing, mocking, or speaking profanity to the Team Leader, client, or team members.

The Team Leader is responsible for bringing closure to the physical healing prayer session and for determining the follow-up strategy for the client. This may include a recommendation to return to Wellsprings of Freedom International for a full freedom session, to read and pray through certain scriptures, or recommending to the client that if they would like to receive additional healing prayer in the future, to sign up for another physical healing prayer session.

The Discerner

The Discerners on a physical healing prayer team are those team members who have been graced with the gift of discerning spirits found in 1 Corinthians 12:10. The Greek phrase used by the apostle Paul in this verse can literally be translated into English as the gift of "distinguishing between spirits" or the ability "to judge between spirits." They are the team's "eyes" and "ears" into the spirit realm. They know the names of demonic spirits that are attacking a client, when an evil spirit is lying, if the demonic spirits are attached to deep emotional wounds in a client's life, and when an evil spirit has left an individual.

The gift of discerning spirits functions in a multitude of ways. Some Discerners see into the spirit realm. Other Discerners overhear in their minds what demons are saying to the client. Still others sense or feel a demonic presence that may be attacking a client or afflicting them physically. Some Discerners may feel overwhelmed by a sense of heaviness, smell evil presences, and see visions or mental pictures. It is possible for the gift of discernment to operate through any of the five senses (including taste on rare occasions).

The gift of discernment is an amazing spiritual gift and, therefore, it comes with much responsibility. As important as the discerning gifts are to a physical healing prayer team, it is imperative that team members understand how this gift can be used improperly and can cause great harm to people if misused. The following is a list of specific guidelines that Wellsprings of Freedom International has established to ensure that the gift of discernment is used correctly and can help bring physical healing to individuals.

The Team Leader is to lead the physical healing prayer session

Even though they are receiving important information from the Holy Spirit, Discerners (and Intercessors) must be careful not to interrupt or interject thoughts without the Team Leader's permission. Biblical advice coming from several different team members at once can be very confusing for the client. Therefore, as the session unfolds, Discerners should wait for direction from their Team Leader as to how the information they are receiving should be shared. This will vary from session to session, depending on the client's ability to hear what the demons are saying to them.

Write everything down

Every Discerner should get into the habit of writing down everything they discern during a physical healing prayer session. Discerners will often see visions, mental pictures, and receive the names of many demonic spirits throughout the session. Writing them down will keep them from being forgotten as the session progresses. Although the Team Leader normally keeps a log of the client's initials, date, what they are asking Jesus for in the session, and if there has been any improvement in their condition (see Appendix A to view the Physical Healing Prayer Session Log Form), the Discerner's notes will be disposed of at the end of each session.

Encourage the client to reveal the demonic lies

It is always best for the client to reveal to the team what the demons are saying and let the Discerners confirm the information. Sometimes demons will lie to the client and the Discerners will then reveal the truth. If a client does not hear the demons speaking, then the Team Leader will give the Discerners instructions about how to pass on or communicate the information to them.

"Love letters" are to be read by the Team Leader or only with the permission of the Team Leader

During a physical healing prayer session, Discerners may receive "love letters" for the client (note that it is possible for Intercessors and Team Leaders to receive "love letters" in a session as well). These are simply words of encouragement, affirmation, and truth that the Discerner senses the Holy Spirit would like to communicate to the client (they are not prophetic words). If and when "love letters" are received, Discerners must not share them verbally with the client, but instead, write them down and hand their notes to the Team Leader. The Team Leader will then confirm and determine whether it falls within the guidelines that Wellsprings of Freedom International has established for testing the spirits (according to 1 John 4:1-3), whether or not it is relevant to the client or session, and if it is to be read during the session. If the worship music ends and the Discerner is not yet finished writing down their "love letter," they should continue writing until it is completed and hand it to the Team Leader before the healing prayer time. A Team Leader may ask the Discerner (or other team member) who received the "love letter" to read it to the client. If pressed for time, the "love letter" can be sent home with the client for them to read after the session is over.

Note that "love letters" are to be used for the encouragement, edification, and instruction of the client. They are not for predicting the future. Nor are they for providing direction about a job, relationship, or any future life decision. Any words or "love letters" that are prophetic in nature are to be disregarded by the Team Leader and not shared with the client. Most "love letters" are filled with Scripture and promises from God's Word about how much He loves the client receiving healing. Any words that are harsh, condemning, or critical should be discarded as well.

The Intercessor

The Intercessor is the spiritual backbone of every physical healing prayer session. They serve as the "power supply" for every WFI team, as they continuously intercede for the client, the Team Leader, the team members, and the session itself. They apply the power and authority of Christ to bring supernatural healing to the client's body. True Intercessors understand that the prayer of a righteous person is powerful and effective (James 5:16).

During the physical healing prayer sessions, the Intercessor praises and worships in the midst of spiritual battle, according to the words of Psalm 149:6-9: "Let the praises of God be in their mouths, and a sharp sword in their hands…" They also pray and ask Jesus to:

1. Provide a spiritual covering of protection over all who are gathered for ministry (the client, Team Leader, Discerners).
2. They pray for the physical, emotional, and spiritual healing of the client.
3. They ask the Holy Spirit to grant wisdom to the Team Leader.
4. They pray for the individual team members who have the gift of discernment, faith, and healing—for greater clarity, wisdom, and understanding.
5. They pray for the names of demonic spirits that are afflicting the client's health to be exposed and revealed during the session.
6. They actively listen to the words spoken by the client, so that they can pray specific prayers for any particular needs that arise throughout the session (if they are experiencing physical pain, etc.).

The Gift of Intercession

When recruiting and forming a physical healing prayer team, we recommend identifying those people in your church, community, or organization who have the gift of intercession. The gift of intercession (prayer) is one of the spiritual gifts that is essential to have on *every* WFI team—including the physical healing prayer teams. It is a vital and powerful gift given to some members of the Body of Christ and to some who actively serve in the Wellsprings of Freedom International ministry. Yet it is often one of the less visible, unnoticed, and underutilized spiritual gifts in the church today.

Interestingly, the gift of intercession is not explicitly mentioned as one of the spiritual gifts listed in Scripture. While there are at least twenty different gifts mentioned in the New Testament (found in the four lists of spiritual gifts in 1 Corinthians 12-14, Romans 12:3-8, Ephesians 4:11-13, and 1 Peter 4:10-11), there are a number of other legitimate spiritual gifts that have been recognized by the Church throughout the last two thousand years of church history. The gift of intercession/prayer is one of those gifts.

What Is the Gift of Intercession?

Simply defined, the gift of intercession is *the special ability that God gives to certain members of the Body of Christ to pray for extended periods of time on a regular basis and allows them to see frequent and specific answers to their prayers to a degree much greater than what is expected of the average Christian.*[1]

Although all Christians are called to pray (it is the privilege and responsibility of every Christian), followers of Jesus Christ who have been graced with the gift of intercession love to pray. They can usually spend extended amounts of time in intense, focused prayer. They enjoy and find great fulfillment in praying for others. They often pray for "divine appointments" and opportunities to pray with others each and every day. True intercessors will tell you that prayer is their passion.

What are Some Signs that You May Have the Gift of Intercession?

Below is a list of ten common signs that may indicate you or another team member has the gift of intercession:

1. You love to spend extended amounts of time praying.
2. You frequently look for opportunities to pray with and for people (at church, at work, at home, etc.).
3. People often seek you out and ask you to pray for them.
4. When you pray, you see God provide inexplicable and miraculous answers to seemingly hopeless and impossible situations.
5. When you pray for people, the Holy Spirit often reveals specific scriptures to pray over them.
6. You believe that God can do the impossible when you pray.
7. God sometimes wakes you up in the middle of the night to pray for people.
8. The Holy Spirit often reveals specific prayers to pray when fighting against demonic strongholds.
9. The people around you affirm and often tell you that you have the gift of intercession.
10. You sometimes see people physically, emotionally, and spiritually healed as you pray.

If a number of these indicators frequently happen or apply to you or another person on your team, then most likely you/they have been equipped with the spiritual gift of intercession.

It is important to realize that no special spiritual gift is needed to have a vital prayer life.[2] However, those who have been given the gift of intercession have an intimate relationship with God that allows them to dwell in the presence of God and to experience breakthroughs, victories, and miracles through the power of prayer.

Like any spiritual gift, a Christ-follower can grow in the gift of intercession. He or she can learn how to develop that gifting and use it powerfully for God's kingdom purposes. By learning to boldly pray God's Word, claim His promises, and pray in accordance with His Word, their prayers will be strengthened in faith and increase in authority.

When learning how to pray more effectively, practice and experience are your best teachers. Like most things in life, *we learn best by doing.* The same is true of intercessory prayer. In addition, finding a more experienced intercessor who can come alongside you and serve as a spiritual mentor will greatly encourage you and enhance the development of your gift.

The Gift of Faith

The gift of faith is another powerful spiritual gift given to some members of the Body of Christ that is utilized effectively in the physical healing prayer sessions. Any team member, whether they be a Team Leader, Discerner, or Intercessor, may have the gift of faith. It can be one of the greatest blessings and sources of encouragement to a physical healing prayer team.

In 1 Corinthians 12:9, the apostle Paul teaches that "the same Spirit gives great faith" to some members of the Body of Christ (NLT). Faith is described here in this list of nine spiritual gifts as one of the manifestations of the Holy Spirit that is given for the "common good" (12:7). Whereas all followers of Jesus Christ have faith in the saving work of Christ, in His ability to move and work in our lives, and to answer prayer, the gift of faith appears to be a special endowment of supernatural faith that can "move mountains" (see Matthew 21:22). It refers to a supernatural conviction that God will reveal His power or mercy in a special way in a specific instance.[3] This kind of extraordinary faith is not something that can be humanly manufactured. It is an assurance given by the Holy Spirit in the core of a person's being that may not make sense to anyone else around them at the time. It is a strong inner confidence that God can do the impossible, work miracles, and move in a powerful way (Mark 9:23).

In a physical healing prayer session, the gift of faith, the gift of intercession, and the gift of healing often function together (see section below on the gift of healing). Those with the gift of faith have a rock-solid confidence in God's ability to heal. It is quite common for team members who have the gift of healing to feel a surge of faith rising up in them during the session in order to pray specific, powerful, and effective prayers over the client (James 5:15-16). In a very real sense, the gift of faith at work in and through the team members builds faith and increases the client's faith that God is about to do something miraculous in and through their body.

Gifts of Healings

In addition to gifts of discernment, intercession, and faith, the gift of healing is a vital spiritual gift that is exercised in the midst of physical healing prayer sessions. As Wellsprings of Freedom International continues to grow and establish new teams in local churches across North America, I (Brian) am being asked more and more questions about the gift of healing and healing ministry. One of the most common questions people often ask is, "How do I know if I have the gift of healing?" These Christ-followers deeply desire to know whether or not God has gifted them with healing gifts. Sadly, however, they tend to be members of churches who either do not teach on or who teach very little about the gift of healing and other related spiritual gifts mentioned in the New Testament.[4]

What Is the Gift of Healing?

Of the more than twenty spiritual gifts explicitly mentioned in the New Testament, one of those gifts discussed in 1 Corinthians 12:9 is the gift of healing: "To one there is given through the Spirit the message of wisdom, to another the message of knowledge by means of the same Spirit, to another faith by the same Spirit, *to another gifts of healing by that one Spirit*, to another miraculous powers, to another prophecy, to another distinguishing between spirits" (1 Corinthians 12:8-10a, NIV).

What most people do not realize is that the Greek phrase used here by the apostle Paul for the gift of healing is in the plural form (Χαρίσματα ἰαμάτων/charismata iamaton). So when translated into English, the phrase should literally read as "gifts of healings," implying that there are many different types of healings (i.e. physical, emotional, mental, or spiritual healings) and/ or that there are many specific occurrences of healings (which we see occurring throughout the book of Acts). Although the miraculous healing of the sick is a major aspect of healing, we should be careful not to limit our understanding of the gift of healing to just mean physical healing. Based on the plural language the apostle Paul uses here in 1 Corinthians 12, some New Testament scholars also suggest that the gift of healing may not actually be a permanent spiritual gift, but a temporary gift bestowed by the Holy Spirit upon a believer at specific times for the healing of another.[5]

It is interesting to observe that in context the apostle Paul sandwiches "gifts of healings" in between the gift of faith and the gift of "miraculous powers." This may also imply some level of overlap between the different spiritual gifts and how they function in the Body of Christ (for example, the gift of faith and the gift of healing working together, the gift of healing and miraculous powers working together, the gift of intercession and the gift of healing operating together, etc.). This has been true in my own personal experience. Sixteen years of experience in the Wellsprings of Freedom International ministry has also confirmed for us that there can be a great deal of overlap between the various spiritual gifts.

In addition, the gift of healing can sometimes manifest in different ways in different people. God may give people with the gift of healing the supernatural ability to minister healing to certain physical conditions or illnesses. For instance, some with the gift of healing may experience consistent breakthroughs and healings when praying for people who are blind, deaf, or mute. Others may experience more regular victories and success when they pray for those suffering from cancer or fibromyalgia. The Holy Spirit may use another believer to consistently bring healing to those battling chronic pain, arthritis, back, knee, leg, and joint pain.

Discovering the Gift of Healing

So how can you know if you have the gift of healing? There are at least five practical ways to help identify whether God has gifted you with this spiritual gift. These include:

1. The "Fruit" Test

The first test is called the "fruit" test. Just like any other spiritual gift (the gift of teaching, leadership, evangelism, faith, etc.), *the areas where you are the most fruitful in ministry often indicate where you are most gifted.* The same is true with the gift of healing. For example, if you lay hands on and pray with people who are sick and suffering from various physical illnesses and they are frequently healed, that is a pretty good indication that you may have the gift of healing. While experience has taught us that not everyone we pray for is physically healed, those who have the gift of healing tend to experience more healings and are used powerfully by the Holy Spirit to minister healing to others. The power isn't theirs. The power is in the Holy Spirit flowing through them and their spiritual gift(s).

The best advice is that if you would like to know if you have the gift of healing, step out in faith and begin to boldly pray for people who are sick, struggling with a physical condition, or another personal issue. Try it and see how God works. You might be amazed at what He does!

2. Confirmation from Others in the Body of Christ

In addition to the "fruit" test mentioned above, one of the most helpful ways to know you are gifted in a certain area is through the affirmation and confirmation of other brothers and sisters in the Body of Christ. While tools such as spiritual gifts tests and inventories are good, they are quite subjective in their approach (we are usually answering questions about ourselves as to how we think we are gifted). However, when others in the church come alongside us and affirm our gifts, it can serve as a powerful confirmation of the way God has designed and gifted us. Therefore, the affirmation of others is a more objective way of helping us discover our spiritual gifts, including the gift of healing. If others recognize God's healing power at work in and through you and see people being healed as a result of your prayers, that can be taken as confirmation that He has probably given you healing gifts.

3. Our God-given Passions and Desires

One of the beautiful truths about all the spiritual gifts is that God oftentimes gifts us in ways that align with our God-given passions and desires. The same is true with the gift of healing. From personal experience, I first discovered that God had bestowed on me the gift of healing while serving on the mission field. I found myself living and serving in a country where people battling sickness, disease, and physical disabilities were all around me. The medical system in our country of service was severely understaffed and underfunded, and because of this, many people chose not to seek out professional medical care. Instead, they preferred their own home remedies and even visited the "babushki" (healers or witch doctors) desperately seeking healing. I was surrounded with physical needs everywhere I went and longed to see Jesus bring miraculous healing to the broken. So I began to cry out to God and ask for the gift of healing. I frequently felt prompted by the Holy Spirit to boldly pray with people for physical and emotional healing, and began to experience God's healing power displayed in miraculous ways. In the context of freedom sessions that I was leading, the Holy Spirit was moving powerfully to bring about deep-level emotional healing and physical healing simultaneously. It seemed like the more I prayed, the more people were being healed! And the more people were being healed, the more joy and sense of fulfillment I experienced in my heart. Through all of these powerful experiences, the Holy Spirit confirmed the gift of healing at work in and through me.

4. Physical Sensations and the Release of Power When We Pray for Healing

There are times when those with the gift of healing experience unusual physical sensations when they are praying for people, such as "hot" sensations, heat flowing through their arms and hands when laying hands on an individual, or tingling sensations. Others with the gift of healing sometimes see or feel God's power literally flowing through the body of an individual, bringing healing to specific areas of the body. Lynette Johnson, who currently leads our physical healing prayer sessions at Wellsprings of Freedom International in Rock Island, Illinois describes the way the gift of healing occasionally operates in and through her:

"For me, my hands sometimes get hot and tingle when I lay hands on the person and pray. I often feel like an electrical current goes through my body, out my arm and hand. Sometimes I physically feel really hot and my ears turn red..."

Different people may experience different physical sensations when they pray for healing. But whenever a person has these kinds of experiences, it is another good indicator that God has gifted them with healing gifts.

5. Spiritual Gifts Tests or Inventories

While under point #2, I mentioned one of the disadvantages of spiritual gifts tests and inventories (in that they can be too subjective at times), there are also some helpful advantages to taking such tests. First of all, spiritual gifts tests and inventories can help a Christian to learn about the rich diversity of gifts discussed in the New Testament. Secondly, they can help new believers to discover some of their God-given gifts so that they can begin to serve in the Body of Christ. Thirdly, the specific questions asked about each spiritual gift, including the gift of healing, can bring clarity and enable a Christian to determine if God has gifted them with this grace/ability. When combined with the first four ways of determining if the Holy Spirit has given you the gift of healing, a spiritual gifts test or inventory can provide additional confirmation and assurance.

Endnotes

1 C. Peter Wagner. *Discover Your Spiritual Gifts: Updated & Expanded* (Ventura, CA: Regal Books , 2005), p . 111.

2 Wagner, p. 57.

3 Gordon D. Fee. *The First Epistle to the Corinthians (NICNT)* (Grand Rapids, MI: Eerdmans Publishing, 1987), p. 593.

4 In some Christian churches and traditions, the gift of healing is referred to as one of the "miraculous" gifts of the Spirit (along with the gifts of signs and wonders, prophecy, tongues, the interpretation of tongues, etc.).

5 Gordon D. Fee. *The First Epistle to the Corinthians (NICNT)*, p. 594.

Chapter 4

Overview of a
Physical Healing Prayer Session

Pre-Session Prayer and Preparation

One of the reasons the physical healing prayer sessions are so powerful is that a great deal of time is spent in prayer, worship, and spiritual preparation long before the client even walks into the session room. Our physical healing prayer teams normally meet one hour before the client comes and the session begins, in order to check in with each team member, pray for one another, and invite the Holy Spirit's presence to come into the room.

Oftentimes, team members have had a busy or stressful day at work, at home, or may be dealing with family issues that are weighing heavily on their hearts and minds. Sometimes, team members may be attacked physically and are struggling with health issues themselves. This hour of prayer and worship beforehand allows the Team Leader to offer pastoral care to their team members and allows the team members to minister to one another in the power and name of Jesus. The result is that the physical pain they are experiencing often disappears, all the distractions of the day are removed from their hearts and minds, and God's peace fills the room. As the worship music plays softly in the background, the team becomes completely focused and ready to begin praying for the client who is in need.

Introduction (the first 20 minutes)

The Wellsprings of Freedom International ministry is based on providing loving, gentle, and compassionate care. Therefore, from the moment a client walks into our building or into the session room, we want our team members to smile, welcome them warmly, and make them feel as comfortable as possible. The Team Leader will usually dim the lighting ahead of time and create a calm, serene, and peaceful atmosphere in the session room. In order to be sensitive to possible allergies that a client may have, we recommend that team members not wear perfumes or cologne when serving in the physical healing prayer sessions. Team members should be aware that some clients may be nervous, fearful, or apprehensive about their session. They may feel embarrassed or ashamed to share about their physical problems. They may have had negative experiences with other healing or deliverance ministries in the past. If they are demonized, the demons that are attacking the client may be angry and afraid that they are coming to their physical healing prayer session for help.

Being aware of these dynamics, the Team Leader should help to ease the client's nerves by talking gently, lovingly, and softly. The Team Leader facilitates the entire session and is the one who will then begin to introduce each team member to the client. Note that there are occasions when a client would prefer to bring a spouse, family member, or close friend to sit in the session with them. However, our policy at Wellsprings of Freedom International is that we do not normally allow spouses, other family members, or friends into the session room with the client. The only exceptions to this rule are parents who are bringing in young children to receive healing prayer, and other WFI team members who are sitting in to observe the physical healing prayer session. The Team Leader is the one who should explain or clarify this policy with the client either beforehand or upon arrival at their physical healing prayer session. Any guests who have come along with the client will be encouraged to spend some time in prayer for the client in our comfortable prayer center or prayer rooms.

Although time is limited, we want the client to get to know something personally about each team member in the room (including what their role will be on the team). By doing this, the team members establish trust with the client and help to calm their fears. During this brief introductory time, it is common for the Team Leader to ask the client if this is their first session at Wellsprings of Freedom International, if they have had a freedom session or physical healing prayer session before, if they have been to a WFI Orientation or training class, and what they know about the WFI ministry. Their response to these questions will help determine how much explanation a Team Leader may need to give to the client.

As a 501c3 nonprofit organization, Wellsprings of Freedom International does require all of its clients to sign a Personal Consent and Liability Waiver form at the beginning of each physical healing prayer session (see Appendix B to view form). The Team Leader is the one who will help explain and/or answer any questions that a client may have about the waiver form at the beginning of the session as well. If the client is a child under the age of eighteen, then a separate Parental Consent & Liability form is also given to a parent or legal guardian (who brings the child to the session) to sign (see Appendix C). Once the waiver is signed, the Team Leader begins to explain to the client what they can expect during the physical healing prayer session and helps to answer any additional questions that a client may have. The Team Leader also asks the client if they are in agreement with the process before beginning. If so, the Team Leader will tell the client that the team members in the room will come into agreement with them on what they are asking Jesus for, and will pray bold prayers for them in Jesus' name (see Matthew 18:19-20 for Jesus' teaching on the power of agreement in prayer).

The Team Leader will then ask the client a series of questions about their physical condition and what they want to be healed of. Some typical questions include:

1. How long have you been in this physical condition?
2. Has the physical condition been diagnosed by a doctor? If so, what was the diagnosis?
3. (If the condition is unknown or unfamiliar to the Team Leader) Could you briefly explain the illness/sickness/disease/condition?
4. Was there something significant going on in your life when the sickness/condition or accident happened? (a stressful or traumatic event, a major life transition, a tragedy, etc.)
5. On a scale of 0 to 10 (10 being the most severe pain), can you rate the pain level you are experiencing and where the pain is?
6. Are you currently taking any medications, including pain medications?

(If the client is currently on medication, then we recommend including a short prayer during the opening prayer time, asking Jesus to work under the effects of any medications.)

During this initial "interview," the Team Leader is writing down what the condition is and any clear guidance or direction from the Holy Spirit on how to specifically pray for the client. While the client is speaking, the Discerners and Intercessor on the team are also beginning to write down their spiritual discernment on paper that will eventually be handed over to the Team Leader. At times, a Team Leader may feel led by the Holy Spirit to share a biblical story that is relevant to the client's situation or a brief testimony of another client who was healed of a similar sickness or condition in their physical healing prayer session in order to encourage the client before they begin to pray.

We have found it to be extremely helpful to get a client to verbalize what they would like Jesus to do for them at the beginning of the session. A Team Leader may even use a story from the Gospels, such as Matthew 20:29-34 where Jesus miraculously heals two blind men and restores their sight. As Jesus was leaving the city of Jericho, these two blind men were sitting by the roadside and shouted out, "'Lord, Son of David, have mercy on us!' Hearing these words, Jesus stopped and called out to them, 'What do you want me to do for you?' 'Lord,' they answered, 'we want our sight'" (20:31-33, NIV). We encourage our Team Leaders to ask the same question of their client that Jesus asked of these two blind men: *What do you want Jesus to do for you?* Allow the client time to answer, to express their desperation and heartfelt desire for healing, and to boldly declare their faith in God's healing power. This increases a client's faith, creates an atmosphere of faith, and sets the spiritual tone for the remainder of the session.

Opening Prayer

Once the introductions are complete, the Team Leader will open with prayer and establish boundaries of protection around the team, the client, and the session room. We recommend the Team Leader set the following boundaries and pray the suggested prayers of protection below, in Jesus' name:

1. Ask the Lord to comfort the client, to help them relax, and to give them His peace (Philippians 4:6-7).
2. Ask the Lord Jesus to stretch out His hand to heal and perform miracles and supernatural healings (Acts 4:30).
3. Let humility fill you as you acknowledge that healing can happen only through the power and authority of Jesus Christ (John 15:5).
4. Ask the Lord to fill the room with His Holy Spirit, and that the room would be considered holy ground (Exodus 3:5).

5. Place the blood covering of Jesus over everyone in the room, including their family members and friends (Exodus 12:21-23).

6. Remind the demons of who Jesus is, that they have already been defeated by Him on the cross, and that they are subject to His authority (Colossians 2:9-10, 13-15).

7. Strictly forbid all demons from manifesting at any time during the session. Remind them that they will respect everyone in the room as children of God, and that there will be no retaliation against the client or team, in Jesus' name.

8. Command all blocking, distracting, and interfering spirits to be cut off from everyone in the room and send them to the feet of Jesus. A Team Leader may also pray against all spirits of Chaos, Vortex, or Whirlwind that may be trying to cause chaos in the client's mind or in the session room.

9. Ask the Lord to elevate the spiritual gifts of everyone in the room, and to provide the team with all the spiritual authority and discernment necessary to bring healing and freedom to the client.

10. Ask the Holy Spirit to reveal and unwrap whatever needs to be unwrapped in this next hour. Ask Him to help the client receive all that He has for them today.

Finally, there may be times when a Team Leader feels led to call on the name of Jehovah-Rapha ("The Lord Who Heals") during the opening prayer time, to begin ministering healing to the client.

Worship

There are a number of reasons why we include a time of musical worship in every physical healing prayer session. We have discovered that worship music is calming for the client and helps to prepare them to receive God's healing touch. Second, experience has taught us that praise and worship is a powerful weapon against the Enemy of our souls and is a great way to enter into spiritual battle. The Enemy is weakened and destabilized by our worship, and it often paves the way for healing and spiritual freedom to occur. Third, during the worship time, the Holy Spirit usually begins to reveal spiritual discernment, "love letters," and information to our Discerners that will be used to provide healing for the client. Fourth, it is quite common for the Holy Spirit to begin healing a client's body while the worship music is playing!

The Team Leader is responsible for choosing the worship music (digital music, CDs) that pertains specifically to physical healing. The Team Leader decides how many songs to listen to, but due to time limitations, will normally listen to 1-2 worship songs. While the worship music is playing, the Discerners on the team are writing down on paper what they are discerning (including visions, pictures, "love letters," names of demonic spirits, etc.). The Discerners are specifically asking the Lord to reveal any spirits that are attacking the client's body or health. Towards the end of the worship time, each Discerner on the team is to hand in their notes to the Team Leader so that they can get a sense of what might be oppressing the client. Note that both Discerners and Intercessors may receive "love letters" and/ or scriptures for the client during the worship time, but all of that information must also be passed to the Team Leader to be used during the rest of the session.

Addressing the Demonics / Deliverance Prayer (next 20 minutes)

After the Team Leader has collected all the notes from their team members, they will then pray and ask the Holy Spirit to reveal the battle plan. If no demonic spirits have been discerned, then the Team Leader can move ahead to the next section (healing prayer). Usually, the next step will be to confront any demonic spirits that may be attacking the client or afflicting their body (which have already been written down on the papers passed to the Team Leaders by the Discerners on the team). At times, a Team Leader will be given a lengthy list of demonic spirits or wounds that may need to be addressed. Note that some Discerners may even see visions of sharp objects, knives, or weapons stuck into the client's body that are causing intense physical pain and suffering.

It is imperative for Team Leaders to understand that in addition to *causing* various forms of sickness, disease, and physical conditions, Satan and his demonic forces of evil can operate in a few other ways as well. For example, demons can exacerbate an existing medical condition, they can intensify the level of pain in a person's body, and/or increase the symptoms of illness. Demonic spirits can also attach themselves to clients through curses placed on them, whether they be curses of witchcraft, word curses spoken against them, self-curses, or generational curses placed on an entire family lineage. Another realm where evil spirits like to play is in the mind. Since demons are liars who work for the "father of lies" (John 8:43-44), they can project lies and negative thoughts into the mind of a sick person, telling them such things as:

"This condition is incurable."
"It's hopeless."
"It's unbearable."
"You can't live like this anymore."
"God will never heal you of this."
"How could God allow this?"
"If God is all-powerful, then why hasn't He healed this?"
"If God is loving, then why…?"
"You're going to die."

The Enemy's wicked lies are intended to ultimately lead a person to a place of hopelessness, depression, and despair. This reality is discussed in more detail in chapter 5 ("The Power of a Diagnosis").

As the Team Leader begins to pray, they will ask Jesus to bind and shackle the demons by name. They will then interrogate some of the strongest demonic spirits, finding out their specific missions and assignments against the client and any lies they have been telling the client. Once the demonic lies have been exposed, the Team Leader will then command the spirits to be silent, in Jesus' name, and ask the Holy Spirit to speak truth to the client in order to replace the Evil One's lies. Once the truth has been spoken, the Team Leader should pray in the name and authority of Christ to cut off all demons that have attached themselves to the client, cancel all of their missions and assignments, command them to leave in Jesus' name, and send them straight to the feet of Jesus. On occasion, a Team Leader may ask Jesus to create a spiritual prison cell and choose to send the demons into the cell to give the client greater assurance that the demonic spirits have left and are now contained. If visions of any sharp objects or weapons are being seen by the Discerners, the Team Leader should also ask Jesus to gently remove those from the client's body and place them into the spiritual prison cell.

Some of the most common demonic spirits encountered in the physical healing prayer sessions include:

Infirmity
Sickness
Death
Pain / Pain Navigator
Hurt
Anxiety / Panic
Health Stealer
Pythos

Breath Stealer
Antichrist
Witchcraft

The Team Leader will check with their Discerners to make sure that all the demonic spirits have been removed. They will also be checking with the client and monitoring how they are feeling. At times, a client may physically feel things moving, shifting, or changing inside their bodies as the demons are being cast out. Other times, a client may begin to feel heat or a hot sensation entering their body or a certain part of their body as God's healing power begins to flow. A Team Leader may even ask the client to do something they weren't able to do before, to see if there is any improvement in their physical condition (i.e., open their hands, stand up, bend over, walk up the stairs, check pain levels, etc.). On occasion, teams have seen clients healed as they try to do what they couldn't do before the session. An example of this happened in Matthew 12:10-13, when Jesus healed a man with a deformed hand. Jesus said to the man, "Stretch out your hand" (12:13). So he stretched out his hand, and it was completely restored, just like the other hand.

A Discerner who faithfully serves in the WFI ministry shared a powerful testimony of this happening in a physical healing prayer session:

"In 2015, I witnessed God's healing grace when I took a young woman from a foreign country, who was staying with me as an exchange student, to Wellsprings of Freedom International. She suffered a physical disability from a hard fall off of a sofa as a one-year-old child. The injury caused a deformity to her left wrist as she grew up and a lack of usage of the entire extremity. She could not straighten her arm at the elbow or oppose her fingers and thumb. Therefore, she could not hold anything in her hand or turn her palm upwards. Due to the lack of mobility and function, she

could not use her arm to do anything and held it tight at her side with the hand resting near her left shoulder.

We witnessed the healing power of Jesus Christ during a physical healing prayer session at WFI. I remember the amazement and raw emotion that each person in the room felt as we watched the young woman be miraculously healed by the power of the Holy Spirit. In complete awe and with tears of joy streaming down our faces, we witnessed this power as the young woman became able to extend her elbow and wrist and then slowly open her hand and turn her palm upwards for the first time. She then held her arms up to praise the Lord! She said she could feel the Lord's healing power moving in her body as He restored mobility to her left arm. After her freedom session the following week, which involved forgiveness, she experienced healing of her wrist, fingers, and thumb. We were all filled with joy as she posed for a picture holding up a pop can, using her fingers and thumb for the very first time!"

There are times during a physical healing prayer session when the Team Leader and Discerners on the team sense that the source of the client's physical condition may be rooted in hurt, pain, and wounds of the past. If this is revealed, then the Team Leader will need to determine if they have enough time to ask Jesus to walk them through an inner healing process (which is outlined in great detail in chapter 9 of "With Gentle Authority"). If time permits, the Team Leader will pray and thoroughly lead the client into an experience of deep-level healing from the wound(s). If time does not permit, the Team Leader will do as much as they can in the physical healing prayer session, finish praying physical healing prayers for the client, and fill and bless the client at the conclusion of the session (see next section below). If lots of wounds are discerned during the session, the Team Leader will strongly recommend that the client come back to Wellsprings of Freedom International for a full (3-hour) freedom session. This will allow the client to experience God's healing at every level—emotional, physical, and spiritual. One former client and cancer survivor experienced deep emotional healing in a freedom session firsthand, as she testified in her own words:

"Not only has God healed me physically from cancer twice, but through prayer during a freedom session, He also healed me emotionally. I no longer feel sadness or fear when I think about all that I went through when I had cancer. It is truly freeing to be prayed over and be set free from those thoughts and feelings!" (J.H.)

Before moving on to the next step, the Team Leader prays and asks Jesus to remove the demonic prison cell and to cleanse the room of any remnants left behind by the Enemy. This is also the time when the Team Leader normally pauses to read any "love letters" that were revealed through the Discerners for the client.

Healing Prayer (final 20 minutes)

The final step will be to pray specific and focused healing prayers over the client. The Team Leader may ask the client's permission to gently touch and/or lay hands on either their shoulder or the top of their head. If led by the Holy Spirit, the Team Leader may ask the client permission to anoint them with oil (usually on top of the head or on the forehead). Sometimes, the Team Leader may ask the client to stand on their feet for a period of time (if they are physically able). The team will then gather around the client to pray in Jesus' name.

The Team Leader will lead the healing prayers that are being spoken over the client. They begin by thanking and praising the Lord for what He is doing and showing the team in the room. They give Him all the honor, glory, and praise in an attitude of worship and thanksgiving (Revelation 4:11, 5:12-13, 7:11-12).

The Team Leader will then shift to praying focused healing prayers over the client's body. While the Team Leader is praying, other team members must be careful not to interrupt or interject their own thoughts and prayers. Often, the Team Leader will stop intermittently to look around at the client and their team members to see if additional or more specific information is being revealed to the Discerners. On occasion, the Team Leader may grant the Discerners or Intercessor permission to pray out loud for the client in turn. This is to allow each team member opportunity to function in their spiritual gifts of healing, faith, and intercession. Sometimes, the Team Leader's prayers may bounce back and forth with the prayers of other team members for a period of time. But all healing prayers must be prayed in a gentle and *orderly* manner.

Some common healing prayers that the Team Leader and/ or team members normally pray include:

1. Asking Jesus to bring everything in the client's body that is out of alignment back into alignment, including their body, soul (mind, will, emotions), spirit, and their entire DNA.
2. Pray that all bodily systems are restored to full function and come back into alignment.
3. A Team Leader may pray targeted prayers for a specific bodily system or organs that have been damaged or compromised (cardiovascular system, immune system, digestive system, kidneys, liver, lungs, knees, joints, etc.).
4. Pray for regeneration of the body or of cells inside the client's body.
5. Command all sickness, infections, disease (i.e. cancer, etc.) to be cut off from its life source and to leave the client's body, in Jesus' name.

As these prayers are prayed and the client's physical condition improves, the Team Leader will continue to pray and speak healing prayers and scriptures over the client in the name of Jesus. For a list of specific healing scriptures that can be prayed over a client, see chapter 8 on page 105, which is titled "Healing Promises Found in Scripture."

The Team Leader should be monitoring and looking at the client to see how they are responding to the healing prayers. For instance, are they feeling hot or a heat sensation? Is a part of their body tingling? Are they crying? The Team Leader will ask the client what is going on if they notice anything unusual happening.

Lynette Johnson tells the following story of a healing in progress... *A client came in for a healing prayer session and shared that she had been hit by a car about thirteen years ago in a car/pedestrian accident. As a result, she had extensive crushing injuries on her left side affecting her shoulder and leg which required a titanium rod and plate. The doctors told her that her body "would never be the same" and "you are lucky to be alive." As she recovered from this accident, she relied more on her right side of her body to compensate for the injuries on the left side. This resulted in her right hip wearing out and the doctors recommended a hip replacement (which she did not get). She recently had a cardiac event where one of her arteries was 98% blocked and received a stent placement. She entered the room walking slowly with the help of a walker. She had been using the walker for four years and was only able to walk without the walker by holding on to furniture. She could only stand/walk for short periods of time. She relied on her husband to help her. The pain level in her right hip was level 1 while sitting and level 4 when standing. But the pain levels would be much higher when grocery shopping, etc. She described some chest pain/heaviness at level 2. The left side of her body she described as feeling "just mild discomfort." As she stood up for prayer, I noticed that she didn't use the walker and she started moving her arms around in the air to check out the range of motion. She was also swaying to the worship music. She had not touched the walker! I asked her to start walking and she asked that the walker be moved away. She was walking on her own now, so we moved the walker out of the room and started walking around the first-floor of the building without any assistance. She was overcome with amazement and joy that she could do this! All the chest pain and heaviness was* gone. *The pain in her right hip was now down to a level 3 and no other pain was noticed in her body. By this time, she had been walking/standing for fifty minutes all on her own! She couldn't wait to tell everyone what Jesus did for her. All praise and glory goes to Jesus!*

Frequently, during a physical healing prayer session, the Holy Spirit will reveal "love letters" for the client being ministered to (as mentioned in chapter 3). In the Wellsprings ministry, we often refer to "love letters" as "pastoral care from the throne of God"—a phrase first coined by Dr. Stephen Seamands. They are powerful reminders of how much God loves the client receiving ministry. If time permits, these "love letters" may be read aloud to the client or given to them to take home to read later.

Filling and Blessing

At the end of each physical healing prayer session, after much demonic oppression has been removed from the client, it is important for the team to pray and ask the Holy Spirit to fill and replace the demons, curses, and lies with truth from God's Word, healing promises, the fruit of the Spirit, and blessings. The Team Leader should ask the Holy Spirit how to pray for the client, and specific information will often be revealed to the Team Leader, Discerners, and/or Intercessor on the team.

The blessings are often the exact opposite of what the client was struggling with. For example, if a person was struggling with feelings of depression or hopelessness over their physical condition, ask the Holy Spirit to fill them with renewed hope and joy (Romans 15:13). If they were battling a terminal disease and were paralyzed by fear, ask Jesus to fill them with His peace and a perfect love that drives out all fear (1 John 4:18). Scripture is filled with ideas of what we can fill and release into a client's life through prayer. The Team Leader should let the Holy Spirit lead and guide them as they pray over the client. They should also check with the Intercessor and Discerners about how God wants to fill the client. When this process is complete, the physical healing prayer session is brought to a close.

Before leaving, the Team Leader likes to ask the client what they think happened in the session today. This gives the client an opportunity to verbalize, declare, and testify that they have been or are being healed in Jesus' name. Giving testimony to what God has done helps to solidify the healing in the client's heart and mind.

Praising God for His Healing

It is important for Team Leaders and team members to realize that some physical healings occur *instantaneously* during the physical healing prayer sessions. When this happens, clients are often overwhelmed with tears of joy and are amazed at how much healing they have received in just one hour! They may thank and even hug the team members for allowing themselves to be empty vessels through which God's healing power can flow. They celebrate together with the team what God has done.

We also know from experience that some physical healings occur *progressively* over time. So if a client isn't feeling any changes in their body, it doesn't mean that God isn't healing them. A client may or may not notice a change in their condition at the end of the session, but a few days, weeks, or months later, they might begin to notice significant levels of healing. The physical healing is a process that God is working in their bodies long after the physical healing prayer session is over.

Some clients are healed as they go from the session. In the hours following their physical healing prayer session, their bodies are being healed and they begin to physically feel the changes occurring. Often the Lord is healing in a process and we don't yet know the outcome in the one-hour session. Or we may never know the outcome. Therefore, we leave it up to the client to make another appointment if they feel the need for more healing prayer. Remember that there were instances when even Jesus had to pray and touch a blind man's eyes twice for them to be completely opened and healed (see Mark 8:22-25).

Lastly, team members and clients must recognize that some healings may be complete (100 percent), while other healings may only be partial (a client's condition may be healed by 50-60 percent). They also need to be open to the possibility that God may not choose to heal the way they are wanting or asking Him to heal at this time, for His own sovereign reasons. Whatever the situation might be, the Team Leader and team members should give praise to God for what He has done, what He is doing, and what He will continue to do in the client's life at the end of the session.

A Note Regarding Time

Team Leaders will discover that one hour goes very quickly. Therefore, to stay on track and keep within the one-hour time frame, Team Leaders must remain focused and keep the introductions, worship, and prayer time moving along. Breaking the sixty minutes down into three twenty-minute blocks (as described above) has proven to be extremely helpful for Team Leaders, recognizing that more or less time may be needed during one of the particular sections. For example, sometimes more time is needed in the introductory part. Sometimes more time is needed during deliverance prayer or the healing prayer section. The Team Leader is the person responsible for ensuring that all three parts of the physical healing prayer session have been accomplished and for finishing the session on time. There are times when a team does go over five or ten minutes in order to complete the session. Because of this possibility, if a team is scheduling back-to-back physical healing prayer sessions with different clients, we highly recommend leaving at least fifteen to thirty minutes in between sessions.

When Ministering to Young Children

When a young child is brought to a session by a parent, grandparent, or legal guardian for physical healing prayer, the Team Leader should be sensitive to their age and speak very calmly, gently, and lovingly to the child throughout the session. If the child is a baby, then we recommend that the parent or grandparent hold the child on their lap during the session. If the child is a toddler or elementary school age and unable to sit still in a chair for an extended period of time, they may also sit on the floor. The Team Leader can provide crayons/markers and a coloring book or sketchpad for the child to color during the session to help keep them focused. In order to avoid making the young child feel afraid and not to overwhelm them, Team Leaders do not normally crowd around, touch, or lay hands on the young child to pray.

As the Team Leader is praying and cutting off any demonic spirits that are attached to the young child and causing physical difficulties, it is quite common for the Discerners on the team to sense that the child is being attacked by generational spirits or curses. If this is the case, then we advise the Team Leader to lead the parent, grandparent, or legal guardian in a thorough prayer, renouncing the specific generational spirits, curses, vows, or dedications aloud in the name of Jesus Christ. By doing this, the parent, who serves in a position of spiritual authority over the child, "stands in the gap" and is able to cut off and remove any evil spirits attached to the child.

Below is a sample prayer that can be prayed aloud in the session:

"In the name of Jesus Christ, I command that all generational, bloodline, and familiar spirits (name specific spirits on list) be bound and shackled and cut off from my child. I further command that all these generational spirits be cut off from all past generations on both the father's and mother's sides of the family, going all the way back to Adam and Eve in the Garden of

Eden. I also cut you off from all present and future generations in this child's family line. I command you, and all others who work with you, to be cut off from my child, in the mighty name of Jesus. All of your missions and assignments against this child are cancelled and destroyed once and for all. I also cancel the power of any vows, curses, or dedications made on behalf of this child. You have no right to my child. Therefore, I command you all to leave them now, and go straight to the feet of Jesus. Amen."

One Final Note Concerning Medications

Wellsprings of Freedom International teams must never tell a client that they should stop taking any type of medication. We must also continue to advise clients to follow through with scheduled surgeries or procedures that have been recommended by doctors. These decisions are to be made between the individual, Jesus, and their medical doctor. WFI physical healing prayer teams are led by well-trained volunteers. We are not trained physicians, psychiatrists, or psychologists. Therefore, we do not give medical advice to clients coming to receive ministry. We also want every client to understand that going to a doctor for medical treatment or taking medication *does not* demonstrate a lack of faith in God's healing power.

Chapter 5

The Power of a Diagnosis

One day, a woman named Sally[1] came to Wellsprings of Freedom desperate for help. Sally was a mother of three beautiful young children, married to a strong Christian husband, and served faithfully in her church on a weekly basis. What I didn't know is that Sally had been diagnosed with stage four breast cancer four months earlier and was told by her doctor that she had only six months to live. After the initial shock of the diagnosis passed, Sally quickly began to spiral downward emotionally into a deep depression. Her spirit was crushed by this unexpected news and she now suffered under the weight of paralyzing fear (for her life, her husband, her children, her family, etc.). She struggled daily with thoughts of utter despair and hopelessness. She had a million questions swirling around her mind and was trying to make sense of it all. Although still a young woman, Sally was now faced with her own mortality. She was also becoming increasingly angry, bitter, and disillusioned with God for allowing this sickness into her life.

Unfortunately, stories like Sally's are all too common. So many clients who come to Wellsprings of Freedom International for ministry have already been diagnosed by a doctor or psychologist/psychiatrist as having a terminal illness, a serious health condition, or some form of mental disorder. They are struggling to pick up the pieces of their shattered lives. Some are suffering from extreme pain. Some have lost all hope that things will ever get better. Still others wonder and doubt if God can even heal their condition.

Over the years, I (Brian) have seen the incredible power that a diagnosis can have over a client. Slowly but surely, a diagnosis can begin to define a client and a client can begin defining themselves by their condition ("You are bipolar," "You have cancer," "You have diabetes," "You are a PTSD victim," etc.). As one client honestly shared with me, *"You refer to the name of the disease—diabetes—as who you are. 'I'm a diabetic.' You classify your abilities by what you're cautioned you can and cannot do because of having this disease. 'I'm going to go blind at a young age,' 'I'm going to have kidney failure at a young age,' or 'I'm going to die at a young age.'"*

It is important to state here that Wellsprings of Freedom International is not opposed to medical doctors or to seeking medical treatment. Nor are we opposed to psychiatry, taking medications, or seeking counseling for various emotional and mental disorders. Our society needs trained medical and mental health professionals to help offer balanced care for the whole person. We deeply respect and give praise to God for raising up quality and competent caregivers who are able to treat some of the most deadliest forms of sickness and disease on the planet.

With that said, we cannot deny or ignore the spiritual/emotional/psychological impact that a diagnosis can potentially have on a client. We know from Scripture that "life and death are in the power of the tongue" (Proverbs 18:21). We are taught as Christians that our words have power—power to bless and power to curse (James 3:9-11). Power to give life and death. Power to offer hope or to destroy hope. Power to build up or to tear down. The same truth applies to a diagnosis spoken directly to a client by a doctor or mental health professional. Depending on how it is spoken and received, a diagnosis can have power to bless or curse, to give life or death, to offer hope or despair to the human spirit.

Listen to the personal testimony of another client who came to our ministry for help: *"I found myself giving into the disease. The more the doctors talked about it and their negative outlook, the more I believed them. I think we are taught at a very early age to look up to doctors, since they have studied and are smarter than we are, and we can believe the lies. Nineteen years ago, I was on three antidepressants just to make it through things, as I wanted to commit suicide. And for years I have suffered back problems because I truly believed the doctors that things could not get better."*

A third client described the ongoing hopelessness she once experienced from a diagnosed condition. Yet God intervened and miraculously healed her of depression. In her own words, she wrote:

"I suffered with 'depression' for twelve years. This diagnosis was given by the doctor and I accepted it. For twelve years, I took medication to keep me from crying, sleeping all the time, and from being 'moody.' I fondly called them my 'happy little blue pills.' They worked pretty good, and of course, I was much nicer to be around. The last year I was taking them, they started to not work as well. So my doctor prescribed me a second medication to boost the first one, which I readily accepted. During that time, I was introduced to the Wellsprings of Freedom ministry for other reasons. After learning about the spiritual realm and how the Enemy attacks us, I started to discern that my diagnosis might not be medical, but rather spiritual in nature. I went to a physical healing prayer session and explained my situation to the team. During the session, it was discerned to be a generational spirit that was attacking me. That day, we cut off all the generational spirits, and from that moment, I knew that I knew that I was HEALED. This was in December, and one of the coldest and dreariest winters we had seen in many years. This was the exact time of year when I struggled the most with my depression. I left that day and went immediately to my doctor so I could be taken off the medications. She was leery, but trusted my instinct. I weaned

off the medications for the next month, and from that moment on, I am still depression free! I no longer take any medications and winters are no longer dreadful to me. PRAISE GOD and the Wellsprings Ministry!"

"Do You Believe that I am Able to do This?"

Whenever I hear stories like this, I am reminded of the story in the Gospel of Matthew, when Jesus encounters two blind men who begged the Lord to have mercy on them. It goes like this…

"As Jesus went on from there, two blind men followed him, calling out, 'Have mercy on us, Son of David!' When he had gone indoors, the blind men came to him, and he asked them, 'Do you believe that I am able to do this?' 'Yes, Lord,' they replied. Then he touched their eyes and said, 'According to your faith let it be done to you'; and their sight was restored. Jesus warned them sternly, 'See that no one knows about this.' But they went out and spread the news about him all over that region. (Matthew 9:27-31, NIV)

In this particular story, two blind men follow after Jesus. They apparently have been in this condition for a long time, yet they cry out; "Son of David, have mercy on us!" (9:27, NLT). Interestingly, this is the very first time in Matthew's Gospel that Jesus is called by this messianic title, "Son of David." The expression refers to the promise of the messianic deliverer who was to come from the line of David, and whose kingdom would never end (2 Samuel 7:12-16, Isaiah 9:7). One of the signs of His coming kingdom was that He would give SIGHT to the blind (see Isaiah 29:18, 35:5, 42:7). The irony is that it is not the Jewish religious leaders, but these two blind men who connect Jesus with the fulfillment of Old Testament prophecy! Jesus is the One who has come to restore sight and cause the blind to see (see Matthew 11:1-6).[2]

What is most fascinating to me is the question that Jesus asks the two blind men: *"Do you believe I can make you see?"* (9:28, NLT). His question challenges their current physical condition. It is a test of their faith. Instead of focusing on their blindness, Jesus wants them to trust in His ability to heal them.

Once they boldly declare their faith in His healing power, Jesus touches their eyes and restores their sight. Because of their faith, Jesus is able to do the impossible. He was able to do what no doctor had been able to accomplish. And these two men went out and told everyone what Jesus had done: "I was once blind, but now I see!"

Every week, at Wellsprings of Freedom International, we are blessed to experience similar stories of miraculous healings. They may not be as dramatic as this one, but we have seen limbs move back into place, eyesight restored, hearing restored, fibromyalgia cured, cancer defeated, and mental illness healed. People who once were taking ten to twelve different medications are now down to one, two, or even no medication! I sometimes wonder how many more people could be healed in our own day if we truly learned to put our faith in Christ's healing power.

Issues Surrounding a Diagnosis

From experience as a Team Leader in the Wellsprings ministry, I have observed at least four key issues that surround a diagnosis given by a medical or mental health professional in the context of a physical healing prayer session (or freedom session). They are:

1. How a diagnosis is received by the client

If a diagnosis has been embraced and received by a client as being *permanent*, it can open the door to all kinds of doubt, fear, worry, anxiety, and depression. Time after time, I have ministered to clients who wholeheartedly believed that what the doctor said will happen. For example, if a doctor told them they have six to twelve months to live, they received it as absolute truth. When a client responds negatively in this manner, the diagnosis can actually function like a curse in their life. This can lead to even more physical, emotional, and spiritual problems and cause the client to fall into an endless cycle of hopelessness and despair. The Enemy then intensifies his work through lies and begins to increase the level of spiritual oppression in the client's life.

2. Renouncing agreements with a diagnosis

If it is revealed in a physical healing prayer session or freedom session that a client has, in fact, believed the condition is permanent, then we often need to lead them through a process of renouncing the agreement that was made with the diagnosis. Rather than embracing the diagnosis and allowing it to define them, we need to help the client speak differently about it. For example, instead of saying "I'm bipolar" or "I'm diabetic," teach them to say "I was diagnosed with bipolar disorder…" or "I was diagnosed with diabetes when I was seven years old." Since the words we use have power, we need to speak them accurately and in a way that doesn't allow the sickness or diagnosis to become a part of our identity. Our identity is found in Christ alone—not in any sickness or disease.

3. Overcoming fear

There is no doubt that fear is one of the greatest struggles most clients who have been diagnosed with a serious condition face. The fears are many—from fear of the future, to fear of what's going to happen to their family/children, to the fear of death. These fears can become paralyzing. They have the power to completely debilitate a client's mind and ability to function normally. Fear is a cruel taskmaster, which can overwhelm and ultimately consume a client.

The first step in helping a client to overcome fear is to help them to renounce the lies associated with the fears ("You're going to die," "God's not going to heal you," "What's going to happen to your children?" etc.). Then, we need to help them internalize the truth in their hearts and minds and speak it out loud. The truth is that God has not given us a spirit of fear, but of power, love, and a sound mind (2 Timothy 1:7). His perfect love casts out all fear (1 John 4:18). Nothing is impossible with God! Everything is possible for those who believe (Mark 9:23). He is a God who forgives all our sins and heals all our diseases (Psalm 103:2-3). Psalm 112:7-8 says, "He will have no fear of bad news; his heart is steadfast, trusting in the LORD. His heart is secure, he will have no fear; in the end he will look in triumph on his foes."

4. Forgiving the doctor or mental health professional

If a client has lost all hope and has been in a deep pit of depression and despair since their condition was diagnosed, they may also need to forgive the doctor who gave the negative diagnosis. The reality is that the words of doctors carry great authority and have the potential to steal life and hope from the client. For example, when a doctor says, "We've done everything we can," "There's nothing more we can do," or "You'll have to live with this for the rest of your life," a client can become angry, bitter, and resentful not just at God, but even at the doctor. This anger, bitterness, resentment, and unforgiveness can give the enemy a legal right to torment and oppress the client.

We must remember that medical doctors are trained to treat what they see. They operate by sight, not by faith. Their entire profession and course of medical treatment is based on empirical evidence. They run series of tests to find out what is wrong with the human body, and based on those test results, they determine appropriate treatment(s). They are doing exactly what they are trained to do and are doing their best to offer quality health care. We praise the Lord for modern technological advances that allows doctors to not only discover, but also treat fatal sicknesses and diseases.

As Christians, on the other hand, we are called to walk by faith, not by sight (2 Corinthians 5:7). It's a completely different way of thinking and living. We are called to believe and trust in the unseen (Hebrews 11:1). This means that just because a doctor said it, doesn't mean it will necessarily happen. There is also the possibility that the initial diagnosis can be wrong (which has happened multiple times to some of our clients). So to surrender to overwhelming fear, worry, and anxiety after a diagnosis is given can be presumptuous and harmful to a Christian's faith.

Restoring Hope

What clients need more than anything when they've been diagnosed with a condition is hope. They need to know that there is hope in any and every situation. So when people come to their physical healing prayer sessions, we ask them what they want Jesus to do for them. Then we come into agreement with them in prayer for the healing. We remind them that He is Jehovah-Rapha, the Lord our Healer (Exodus 15:13). We know that Jesus can heal in many different ways and that the healing is ultimately in His hands and His timing.

At the same time, we do not tell anyone to stop taking their medications, to stop seeing doctors, or not to have necessary surgeries. We know that Jesus can heal using modern medicine as well. How and when He decides to heal is ultimately up to Him.

If there have been word curses spoken against the client, we cut them off, in Jesus' name. If Discerners on the team see demonic spirits attached to the physical condition, they are removed in the name of Jesus. We then ask and pray in faith for a miracle. We continually give God the glory, honor, and praise in advance for what He is going to do.

Finally, we try to equip the client to win the spiritual battles that are raging in their mind. Since coping with a serious mental or physical condition can sometimes be an emotional roller coaster, it is essential to learn how to stand in victory on a daily basis. Time after time, I have seen clients overcome impossible odds and rise above their circumstances. They have chosen to maintain a positive and hopeful outlook, finding refuge in God's Word and putting their hope in His promises on a daily basis. They have learned how to gain victory in their minds (by rebuking the fears and the Enemy's lies), which allows them to effectively manage their emotions. A helpful verse for clients to consider is Proverbs 23:7, which says; "For as he thinks in his heart, so is he" (AMP). What a person thinks has a profound influence over how they feel, regardless of the severity of the sickness or condition.

In Acts 5, Luke tells us that the apostles performed many miraculous signs and wonders among the people (5:12). More and more men and women believed in the Lord and the early Christian community was increasing in number. As a result, people brought the sick into the streets and laid them on beds and mats so that at least Peter's shadow might fall on them as he passed by. Large crowds gathered from the towns around Jerusalem, bringing their sick and those tormented by evil spirits, and all of them were healed (5:13-16).

I sometimes wonder how many of these people were told that their physical and mental conditions were permanent. I also wonder how long they were suffering from these various infirmities, sicknesses, and diseases. Unfortunately, Luke's narrative doesn't offer those details. What we do know is that all those who were sick and tormented by evil spirits were healed in the name of Jesus!

The apostles gave powerful testimony that Jesus Christ is the Great Physician. His healing power can mend what is broken and restore us to health. There is no disease that He cannot heal. There is no malady that can't be made well. He alone holds the keys to life and death (Revelation 1:18). He alone has the power to heal. And He alone can change seemingly impossible situations. May we come to Him in faith and boldly approach His throne of grace with confidence (Hebrews 4:16)!

Endnotes

1 A fictitious name and story is used here to protect the identity of our clients, although the story is based on true experiences at Wellsprings of Freedom International.

2 Wilkins, Michael J. NIV *Application Commentary, New Testament: Matthew* (Grand Rapids, MI: Zondervan, 2004), p. 372.

Chapter 6

Walking in Your Healing

At the end of each physical healing prayer session, the Team Leader will sometimes offer practical advice and suggestions to the client on how to continue walking in their healing. If a client has experienced miraculous healing or some level of physical healing during the session, we want to equip them to stand firm and to live in that place of healing. Learning to "walk by faith, not by sight" (2 Corinthians 5:7), as well as trusting and believing God for complete healing, is an essential truth that we try to help every client understand.

Below are a number of steps that can be taken and/or helpful tips that can be shared with a client to encourage them before they leave their physical healing prayer session.

Put on the full armor of God daily (Ephesians 6:10-19)

After their sessions, one thing clients need to keep in mind is that the Enemy may try to cause doubt and "steal" their healing if they aren't careful. Satan does this primarily through lies that he projects into our minds—lies of doubt, lies of fear, lies of hopelessness and despair, and lies that God did not or cannot heal. He can also accomplish his task through questions in our minds, such as "Did God really heal you?" "You're not going to believe this stuff, are you?" "Do you really think that God has the power to heal cancer?", etc. Thus, the client still has some responsibility to war against these negative thoughts and lies after the session is over. By *daily* putting on the full armor of God (the belt of truth, the breastplate of righteousness, the sandals of peace, the shield of faith, the helmet of salvation, the sword of the Spirit), the client can be empowered by the Holy Spirit and covered in God's protection against the devil's schemes.

Clients must beware of and recognize the lies of the Enemy or physical symptoms that may try to come back (pain, sickness, etc.). The Enemy may even attempt to tell them that "nothing happened" during their session(s) and may try to place the same symptoms back on them. For example, if a client was healed of chronic lower back pain in their session, and a week later, a little bit of pain begins to be felt in that same area, it is important for a client not to allow doubt and unbelief to creep and convince them that "God didn't heal" or that "the session didn't help." The client needs to learn how to reject these lies and stand their ground. One of the best ways to overcome the Enemy's lies is to go to war with the Word of God. They can be encouraged to boldly declare the truth that God has healed and is healing their body.

Meditate on any scriptures and/or "love letters" that were given during the session

Oftentimes, during the physical healing prayer sessions, the Holy Spirit will reveal specific scriptures or "love letters" for the client. These truths and words of encouragement usually bring tremendous healing to the client and restore hope. The scriptures and "love letters" that are spoken and shared during the physical healing prayer session can be written down and handed to the client for them to take home with them and keep in a journal. Clients are advised to read, reflect, and meditate on those scriptures and/or "love letters" whenever they are in need of a reminder of what God did during the session. The scriptures that are revealed can also be used in prayer against the Enemy as a powerful spiritual weapon. Hebrews 4:12 tells us that the Word of God is alive and powerful. It is sharper than the sharpest two-edged sword. It is our greatest offensive weapon against the Evil One.

If the condition has improved during the session, but not completely, encourage the client to continue thanking and praising God for what He has already done.

Scripture teaches us that praise is another powerful weapon against the Enemy. Praise and worship has the power to lift us above our (physical) circumstances so that we can live in spiritual and emotional freedom. We have observed that more healing seems to occur in an atmosphere of thankfulness and praise. So if a client has experienced some healing during their physical healing prayer session, they should continue to thank Jesus, press in, and ask Him for more. Reassure them that God often responds to a person's faith (see James 5:15-16). Urge them to ask God for complete healing. Remind them that all things are possible for those who believe (Mark 9:23).

Remind the client of the importance of the words they speak

As mentioned in chapter 5 ("The Power of a Diagnosis"), the words we speak have power over us (see Proverbs 18:21). Therefore, clients may need to be instructed to speak differently about their condition or sickness when they leave their physical healing prayer session. Rather than "owning" the condition and allowing their sickness or disease to define them, they should be encouraged to change the language they use and the words they speak when talking about themselves or their health to others.

Be careful who they share the healing with

The reality is that other people's negative words or unbelief can affect the client once they walk out of the session room. Because the words others speak to us can also have power—to give life or steal life, to bring healing or to cause hurt and pain—clients should exercise wisdom in who they freely share their story and testimony with. Well-meaning family members may not believe that God still miraculously heals today. Friends may cast doubt about the healing that has taken place, which may cause the client to doubt and question what Christ has done. Co-workers may be skeptical of the Wellsprings of Freedom International ministry altogether, and may naively believe that the client has gotten involved with some kind of "cult." Whatever the case may be, it is important for the client to testify about their healing. They just need to testify to the right people! At Wellsprings of Freedom International, the Team Leader sometimes has the client who is miraculously healed during a session immediately go and tell the leaders of WFI what the Lord has done.

Maintain a healthy and balanced lifestyle

After their physical healing prayer sessions is over, a client will still need to keep fit spiritually, emotionally, mentally, and physically. This is true for every follower of Jesus Christ. Discipline is an essential part of the Christian life (1 Timothy 4:7-8) and self-control is described as a fruit of the Spirit (Galatians 5:22-23). Any bad or unhealthy habits that contributed to the physical condition (eating, smoking, lack of exercise, etc.) should be changed as soon as possible to help the client live and walk in long-term healing. If the physical condition was caused by the client's own poor lifestyle choices, and God heals them, but they refuse to change those bad habits and make righteous, God-honoring choices, they may open themselves back up to the same problem(s) again. If sin was the cause for the sickness or condition, then it is imperative that the client repent, walk in obedience to God, and stay away from willful sin. We see a biblical example of this in John 5:14, when after Jesus healed a man who had been an invalid for thirty-eight years, his message to him was: "See, you are well again. Stop sinning or something worse may happen to you." If the client goes back to doing whatever caused the sickness, then it is reasonable that the condition could return again in the future.

Keep short accounts and walk in forgiveness

Unforgiveness is a legal right that Satan uses to lead us into spiritual, emotional, and physical bondage. Therefore, clients need to be careful not to harbor anger, bitterness, resentment, and unforgiveness in their hearts against those who hurt them, and to not give the devil a foothold in their lives (Ephesians 4:26-27). Unforgiveness is like a poison that ultimately affects every part of our being—spiritual, emotional, and physical. It can be compared to an infection that spreads and only causes more hurt and pain in our lives. Learning the habit of being "quick to listen, slow to speak, and slow to become angry" (James 1:19-20) will help prevent clients from openly inviting Satan and his demonic forces back into their lives to torment them. If a demonic spirit(s) played a part in the physical condition, it is important that the client not open up any doors for the spirit(s) to enter back in.

Hand the client a "Continuing the Journey Toward Freedom" follow-up booklet, if they do not yet have one

Wellsprings of Freedom International has published a short follow-up booklet for this very purpose—to better equip clients to walk in long-term healing and freedom. This booklet is filled with truth from God's Word and useful information on spiritual warfare, God's protection, and the power of forgiveness. It also includes suggested prayers that a client can pray when they feel attacked in the future. Copies of "Continuing the Journey Toward Freedom" can be purchased online at www.wellspringsoffreedom/store or through our Wellsprings of Freedom office at office@wellspringsoffreedom.net.

Sign-up to become a member of the "Splashes From Wellsprings" discipleship website

In addition to the "Continuing the Journey Toward Freedom" follow-up booklet, WFI has also created an online discipleship website, called "Splashes From Wellsprings" (www.splashesfromwellsprings.com), to empower clients to maintain their healing and newfound freedom. "Splashes From Wellsprings" is a powerful, user-friendly discipleship resource that can be accessed 24/7 whenever a client is in need of spiritual encouragement. Clients can be encouraged to sign up and become a member of "Splashes" at the end of each physical healing prayer session.

A client may make an appointment for another physical healing prayer session

If a client has received a level of physical healing in their first session, but feels like they could still greatly benefit from another (second) physical healing prayer session, they can contact the WFI office at (309) 788-8100 or e-mail at office@wellspringsoffreedom.net to schedule another appointment. It is important to note that at WFI, most clients do not receive more than two physical healing prayer sessions in a calendar year. The leaders of WFI will ultimately determine if any exceptions are to be made to this policy in extreme cases and circumstances.

Chapter 7

Theological Tensions in Healing Ministry

Over the last decade, I (Brian) have had the privilege of witnessing all kinds of extraordinary healings—physical, spiritual, and emotional. Those suffering from advanced-stage cancer, fibromyalgia, food allergies, and severe depression were miraculously healed! Others were delivered from severe chronic pain. Yet over that same decade, I have also lost a number of close family members and friends to death. In all of these instances, we prayed earnestly, fasted, and pleaded for God to heal. Some were miraculously healed, while others were not. Some of these people are "walking miracles" and have gone on to live normal lives again. While others have peacefully entered into the arms of Jesus for the rest of eternity.

All of these experiences have led me to the conclusion that there is a great deal of *irony* and *theological tension* in healing ministry. There are no easy answers to such a complex issue as divine healing. Being in leadership of a healing ministry such as Wellsprings of Freedom International forces me to wrestle with these theological questions and tensions on a daily basis.

Below are four theological tensions and lessons that I have learned over the years concerning physical healing. My hope and prayer is that these biblical truths will encourage you and bring clarity to your own heart and mind as you seek to learn more about how God heals.

The Bible makes it clear that all our days are numbered

In Psalm 139:16, King David writes, "…all the days ordained for me were written in your book before one of them came to be" (NIV). This psalm teaches us that God not only created our bodies, but He also determines the length of our days. Therefore, we can rest assured that no one or nothing can cut them short. Our lives are ultimately in His hands. *Healing is also ultimately in His hands.* No amount of medication or life support can alter what God has planned. And no amount of faith can heal, if God has chosen to call someone home. He alone holds the keys to life and death (Revelation 1:18). Thus, He alone decides when a person is healed (either temporarily here on earth or eternally in heaven).

Psalm 90:10 reminds us, "The length of our days is seventy years—or eighty, if we have the strength; yet their span is but trouble and sorrow, for they quickly pass, and we fly away" (NIV). Life is short and our time here on earth passes quickly. As the prophet Isaiah poetically expresses, "All life is like the grass. All of its grace and beauty fades like the wild flowers in a field. The grass withers, the flower fades as the breath of the Eternal One blows away. People are no different from grass. The grass withers, the flower fades; nothing lasts except the word of our God. It will stand forever" (Isaiah 40:6b-8, The Voice).

We tend to forget that everyone Jesus healed eventually died

One of the consequences of the Fall (recorded in Genesis 3) is that our human bodies are now subject to sickness, disease, pain, and death. This was not part of God's original plan for humanity, but it is the harsh reality of sin entering the world. As a result, the Scriptures make it clear that we are all mortal human beings who will eventually die.

Throughout the Gospels, we read how Jesus miraculously healed many. He opened the eyes of the blind, healed the sick, raised the dead, and cleansed those who suffered from leprosy. His miracles of healing amazed the crowds. They were powerful testimonies and signs of God's kingdom coming to earth. What we often forget, however, is that *everyone Jesus healed also eventually died.* These physical healings were only temporary. They may have extended one's life several years and/or significantly increased the quality of one's life on earth, but all who were physically healed were eventually called home.

We see an example of this in the life of King Hezekiah. In Isaiah 38 and 2 Kings 20, we read how Hezekiah became ill and was close to the point of death. The prophet Isaiah then delivers a message from the Lord to the king, stating, "This is what the LORD says: Put your house in order, because you are going to die; you will not recover" (Isaiah 38:1, NIV). When King Hezekiah heard this news, he turned his face to the wall and pleaded to the Lord. He broke down and wept bitterly (38:2-3). In response to Hezekiah's cries, the Lord was gracious and merciful, and announced to the king that he would add fifteen years to his life (38:5). God gave King Hezekiah an extension on life. But his healing was only temporary. Hezekiah eventually died like all the other Old Testament kings of Judah and Israel (2 Kings 20:21).

One of the great ironies in healing ministry is that even the greatest "faith healers" of the last century all died. For example, John Wimber, founder of the Vineyard Movement, had a powerful healing ministry during the 1980s and 1990s. God used Wimber powerfully to perform miraculous signs and wonders and to heal many physical afflictions at various worship services and conferences across North America. Yet in 1997, John Wimber tragically died of a *brain hemorrhage* at age sixty-three. Although the Lord used him mightily to bring healing to thousands, Wimber himself eventually passed away at a relatively young age. This is part of the irony and tension we sometimes experience in healing ministry.

Why God chooses to heal some and not everyone is a divine mystery

It seems like the two questions I have been asked more than any other in the Wellsprings ministry are: "Why doesn't God still heal?" or "Why didn't God heal when…?" In their hearts, most clients who come to Wellsprings with physical problems long for Jesus to heal them physically. But in their minds, many are often plagued with doubt, fear, and confusion—wanting to believe that God will heal, but afraid that He won't. If the Lord does not heal them physically (even though He does heal them emotionally and spiritually), they sometimes begin to ask all the "why" questions. This is yet another tension we experience in a healing ministry like Wellsprings of Freedom International. Unfortunately, there are no easy answers or explanations.

I once read an interview between Bill Johnson and Randy Clark, who serve at Bethel Church (in Redding, California) and Global Awakening respectively. Both Johnson and Clark serve in and lead powerful healing ministries in their local church and around the world. I was fascinated by a statement that Randy Clark made during the interview. Back when he began his healing ministry, Clark explains;

"I really started to pay attention to the numbers. I figured that in the United States back at that time, out of the total number of people present, we'd see about 10 percent minimum healed (this took place prior to the last few years, during which we've seen a much bigger breakthrough)… I would start making this declaration almost everywhere I went. I knew 10 percent of the people there would get healed, and the way I knew was that I had always been counting the numbers, as I said. And there had always been at least 10 percent; that's the minimum. So I got up and declared (one night in meeting of 8,000 people in Brazil), 'Before we leave tonight, there will be at least eight hundred people who get healed.'... That's simply the minimum number we've been seeing."[1]

What struck me here is that even a thirty-year veteran in healing ministry acknowledges that for many years, only about ten percent of those who attended his meetings and services were physically healed. If one hundred people showed up at a meeting, then around ten would be healed. If one thousand people attended, then around one hundred were healed. This means that the other nine hundred were not necessarily physically healed and may have walked away in the same condition as when they came.

Our experience in the Wellsprings of Freedom ministry seems to be fairly similar, although the statistics may differ a bit. Wellsprings of Freedom International averages about an 85 percent success rate with emotional and spiritual healings in freedom sessions. Our physical healing percentage rate is slightly lower, but around 50–60 percent of our clients do testify to some area of physical healing as a result of their physical healing prayer sessions.

Certainly, not everyone who comes in for physical healing prayer sessions is miraculously healed. The reasons why God chooses to heal some and not others are many. *Healing is ultimately a divine mystery that is often beyond human explanation.* The truth is that Scripture has not called us to explain sickness and healing; it only calls us to pray for and to heal the sick.[2]

Some clients who come to WFI for ministry each month are miraculously healed. We see the changes with our own eyes and the clients physically feel the changes happening in their bodies. We hear their testimonies often and doctors are able to confirm the miraculous healings afterwards. These clients then go out and tell the world how much Jesus has done for them. More often than not, they are amazed at what the Lord has done!

Rather than dwelling on those who are not healed and speculating on the deeper theological questions as to why God doesn't heal, we choose to celebrate the healings that do occur and give praise to God for displaying His glory and power in their lives. To use a modern colloquialism... In healing ministry the glass can either be "half empty" or "half full." We can either dwell on all those who are not healed (and try to figure out the reasons why), or dwell on all those who are healed. At Wellsprings of Freedom International, we choose to view the glass as always being "half full."

One day, our bodies will experience complete healing

As mentioned above, even though the physical healings that human beings experience on earth are temporary, we all look forward to the time when one day, we will be completely and eternally healed. When that day comes, we will all be *permanently healed*. We will all be given a new and resurrected body (1 Corinthians 15:35-57). Our bodies and all of creation that now groan as in the pains of childbirth eagerly await their redemption (Romans 8:18-23). Our bodies will again be free from death and decay. They will no longer be subject to sickness and disease. They will be glorified bodies, released from sin and suffering. Oh, how we long for that glorious day! For many, that day can't come soon enough.

To those who wrestle with the tensions in healing ministry and struggle to understand the mystery of divine healing, I want to share with you an important truth that the Holy Spirit has taught me over the years: *God always heals!* The question is not if God heals, but *when* God heals. Will He choose to heal this side of heaven—to temporarily heal here on earth? Or will He choose to heal on the other side—to permanently heal in heaven? When God heals an individual of a physical infirmity, we will celebrate and praise Him. When God completely heals an individual and calls them home into His arms, we will celebrate and praise Him. As I learned many years ago, healing is God's business. How and when He chooses to heal is ultimately up to Him. Our job as Christians is to fervently pray, fast, and ask in faith for healing, believing that God can do the impossible (Mark 9:23). We press in, earnestly pray for those who are sick, and leave the results to God.

Endnotes

1 Bill Johnson & Randy Clark. *Healing Unplugged: Conversations and Insights from Two Veteran Healing Leaders* (Grand Rapids, MI: Chosen Books, 2012), pp. 80-81.

2 Ken Blue. *Authority To Heal* (Downers Grove, IL: InterVarsity Press, 1987), Location 1368.

Chapter 8

Healing Promises Found in Scripture

God's Word is filled with promises of healing. Below is a list of scriptures that remind us of God's healing power in our lives. Some of these scriptures may be read, quoted, and/or prayed over clients during the physical healing prayer sessions. Clients can be encouraged to read and pray through particular scriptures listed here. This chapter can also serve as a helpful reference guide for Team Leaders during a session.

> "There the LORD issued a ruling and instruction for them and put them to the test. He said, 'If you listen carefully to the LORD your God and do what is right in his eyes, if you pay attention to his commands and keep all his decrees, I will not bring on you any of the diseases I brought on the Egyptians, for I am the LORD, who heals you." (Exodus 15:25-26, NIV)

> "And the Lord will protect you from all sickness. He will not let you suffer from the terrible diseases you knew in Egypt, but he will inflict them on all your enemies!" (Deuteronomy 7:15, NLT)

> "See now that I myself am he! There is no god besides me. I put to death and I bring to life, I have wounded and I will heal, and no one can deliver out of my hand." (Deuteronomy 32:39, NIV)

"Then he went out to the spring and threw the salt into it, saying, 'This is what the Lord says: I have healed this water. Never again will it cause death or make the land unproductive.'" (2 Kings 2:21, NIV)

"Have mercy on me, Lord, for I am faint; heal me, LORD, for my bones are in agony." (Psalm 6:2, NIV)

"LORD my God, I called to you for help, and you healed me." (Psalm 30:2, NLT)

"Let all that I am praise the Lord; with my whole heart, I will praise his holy name. Let all that I am praise the LORD; may I never forget the good things he does for me. He forgives all my sins and heals all my diseases. He redeems me from death and crowns me with love and tender mercies. He fills my life with good things. My youth is renewed like the eagle's!" (Psalm 103:1-5, NLT)

"He sent out his word and healed them; he rescued them from the grave." (Psalm 107:20, NIV)

"The LORD builds up Jerusalem; he gathers the exiles of Israel. He heals the brokenhearted and binds up their wounds." (Psalm 147:2-3, NIV)

"Trust in the LORD with all your heart; do not depend on your own understanding. Seek his will in all you do, and he will show you which path to take. Don't be impressed with your own wisdom. Instead, fear the LORD and turn away from evil. Then you will have healing for your body and strength for your bones." (Proverbs 3:5-8, NLT)

"My child, pay attention to what I say. Listen carefully to my words. Don't lose sight of them. Let them penetrate deep into your heart, for they bring life to those who find them, and healing to their whole body." (Proverbs 4:20-22, NLT)

"Some people make cutting remarks, but the words of the wise bring healing." (Proverbs 12:18, NLT)

"Surely he took up our pain and bore our suffering, yet we considered him punished by God, stricken by him, and afflicted. But he was pierced for our transgressions, he was crushed for our iniquities; the punishment that brought us peace was on him, and by his wounds we are healed." (Isaiah 53:4-5, NIV)

"'I have seen their ways, but I will heal them; I will guide them and restore comfort to Israel's mourners, creating praise on their lips. Peace, peace, to those far and near,' says the Lord. 'And I will heal them.'" (Isaiah 57:18-19, NIV)

"Heal me, Lord, and I will be healed; save me and I will be saved, for you are the one I praise." (Jeremiah 17:14, NIV)

"Why do you cry out over your wound, your pain that has no cure? Because of your great guilt and many sins I have done these things to you. 'But all who devour you will be devoured; all your enemies will go into exile. Those who plunder you will be plundered; all who make spoil of you I will despoil. But I will restore you to health and heal your wounds,' declares the Lord, 'because you are called an outcast, Zion for whom no one cares.'" (Jeremiah 30:15-17, NIV)

"It was I who taught Ephraim to walk, taking them by the arms; but they did not realize it was I who healed them." (Hosea 11:3, NIV)

"But for you who fear my name, the Sun of Righteousness will rise with healing in his wings. And you will go free, leaping with joy like calves let out to pasture. On the day when I act, you will tread upon the wicked as if they were dust under your feet," says the Lord of Heaven's Armies." (Malachi 4:2-3, NLT)

"Jesus went throughout Galilee, teaching in their synagogues, proclaiming the good news of the kingdom, and healing every disease and sickness among the people. News about him spread all over Syria, and people brought to him all who were ill with various diseases, those suffering severe pain, the demon-possessed, those having seizures, and the paralyzed; and he healed them." (Matthew 4:23-24, NIV)

"Suddenly, a man with leprosy approached him and knelt before him. 'Lord,' the man said, 'if you are willing, you can heal me and make me clean.' Jesus reached out and touched him. 'I am willing,' he said. 'Be healed!' And instantly the leprosy disappeared." (Matthew 8:2-3, NLT)

"Then Jesus said to the centurion, 'Go! Let it be done just as you believed it would.' And his servant was healed at that moment." (Matthew 8:13, NIV)

"When evening came, many who were demon-possessed were brought to him, and he drove out the spirits with a word and healed all the sick." (Matthew 8:16, NIV)

"She said to herself, 'If I only touch his cloak, I will be healed.' Jesus turned and saw her. 'Take heart, daughter,' he said, 'your faith has healed you.' And the woman was healed at that moment." (Matthew 9:21-22, NIV)

"Jesus traveled through all the towns and villages of that area, teaching in the synagogues and announcing the Good News about the Kingdom. And he healed every kind of disease and illness." (Matthew 9:35, NLT)

"That evening after sunset the people brought to Jesus all the sick and demon-possessed. The whole town gathered at the door, and Jesus healed many who had various diseases. He also drove out many demons, but he would not let the demons speak because they knew who he was." (Mark 1:32-34, NIV)

"When they heard about all he was doing, many people came to him from Judea, Jerusalem, Idumea, and the regions across the Jordan and around Tyre and Sidon. Because of the crowd he told his disciples to have a small boat ready for him, to keep the people from crowding him.

For he had healed many, so that those with diseases were pushing forward to touch him." (Mark 3:8-10, NIV)

"And wherever he went—into villages, towns or country-side—they placed the sick in the marketplaces. They begged him to let them touch even the edge of his cloak, and all who touched it were healed." (Mark 6:56, NIV)

"At sunset, the people brought to Jesus all who had various kinds of sickness, and laying his hands on each one, he healed them." (Luke 4:40, NIV)

"Yet the news about him spread all the more, so that crowds of people came to hear him and to be healed of their sick-nesses." (Luke 5:15, NIV)

"He went down with them and stood on a level place. A large crowd of his disciples was there and a great number of people from all over Judea, from Jerusalem, and from the coastal region around Tyre and Sidon, who had come to hear him and to be healed of their diseases. Those trou-bled by impure spirits were cured, and the people all tried to touch him, because power was coming from him and healing them all." (Luke 6:17-19, NIV)

"But the crowds learned about it and followed him. He wel-comed them and spoke to them about the kingdom of God, and healed those who needed healing." (Luke 9:11, NIV)

"When you enter a town and are welcomed, eat what is offered to you. Heal the sick who are there and tell them, 'The kingdom of God has come near to you.'" (Luke 10:8-9, NIV)

"And a great crowd of people followed him because they saw the signs he had performed by healing the sick." (John 6:2, NIV)

"By faith in the name of Jesus, this man whom you see and know was made strong. It is Jesus' name and the faith that comes through him that has completely healed him, as you can all see." (Acts 3:16, NIV)

"Now, Lord, consider their threats and enable your servants to speak your word with great boldness. Stretch out your hand to heal and perform signs and wonders through the name of your holy servant Jesus." (Acts 4:29-30, NIV)

"Crowds gathered also from the towns around Jerusalem, bringing their sick and those tormented by impure spirits, and all of them were healed." (Acts 5:16, NIV)

"Therefore confess your sins to each other and pray for each other so that you may be healed. The prayer of a righteous person is powerful and effective." (James 5:16, NIV)

"When they hurled their insults at him, he did not retaliate; when he suffered, he made no threats. Instead, he entrusted himself to him who judges justly. 'He himself bore our sins' in his body on the cross, so that we might die to sins and live for righteousness; "by his wounds you have been healed." (1 Peter 2:23-24, NIV)

"Dear friend, I pray that you may enjoy good health and that all may go well with you, even as your soul is getting along well." (3 John 2, NIV)

"Then the angel showed me the river of the water of life, as clear as crystal, flowing from the throne of God and of the Lamb down the middle of the great street of the city. On each side of the river stood the tree of life, bearing twelve crops of fruit, yielding its fruit every month. And the leaves of the tree are for the healing of the nations. No longer will there be any curse…" (Revelation 22:1-3a, NIV)

Scriptures Relating to Infertility

"God blessed them and said to them, 'Be fruitful and increase in number; fill the earth and subdue it.'" (Genesis 1:28, NIV)

"Then God blessed Noah and his sons, saying to them, 'Be fruitful and increase in number and fill the earth.'" (Genesis 9:1, NIV)

"Then the Lord said to Abraham, 'Why did Sarah laugh and say, "Will I really have a child, now that I am old?" Is anything too hard for the Lord? I will return to you at the appointed time next year and Sarah will have a son.'" (Genesis 18:13-14, NIV)

"Then God remembered Rachel; he listened to her and opened her womb. She became pregnant and gave birth to a son and said, 'God has taken away my disgrace.' She named him Joseph, and said, 'May the Lord add to me another son.'" (Genesis 30:22, NIV)

"Worship the Lord your God, and his blessing will be on your food and water. I will take away sickness from among you, and none will miscarry or be barren in your land. I will give you a full life span." (Exodus 23:25-26, NIV)

"If you pay attention to these laws and are careful to follow them, then the Lord your God will keep his covenant of love with you, as he swore to your forefathers. He will love you and bless you and increase your numbers. He will bless the fruit of your womb, the crops of your land, your grain, new wine and oil, the claves of your herds and the lambs of your flocks in the land that he swore to your forefathers to give you. You will be blessed more than any other people none of your men or women will be childless, nor any of your livestock without young." (Deuteronomy 7:12-15, NIV)

"But to Hannah he gave a double portion because he loved her, and the Lord had closed her womb. And because the Lord had closed her womb, her rival kept provoking her in order to irritate her. This went on year after year... So in the course of time Hannah conceived and gave birth to a son.

She named him Samuel, saying: 'Because I asked the Lord for him.'" (1 Samuel 1:5-6, 20, NIV)

"Michal, David's wife, was accusing and mocking in disgust with King David, when her husband was dancing before the Lord. As a result of this Michal, the daughter of Saul, remained childless throughout her entire life." (2 Samuel 6:20-23)

Scriptures Relating to the Deaf and Mute

"Jesus left there and went along the Sea of Galilee. Then he went up on a mountainside and sat down. Great crowds came to him, bringing the lame, the blind, the crippled, the mute and many others, and laid them at his feet; and he healed them." (Matthew 15:29-30, NIV)

"Then will the eyes of the blind be opened and the ears of the deaf unstopped." (Isaiah 35:5, NIV)

"People were overwhelmed with amazement. 'He has done everything well,' they said. 'He even makes the deaf hear and the mute speak.'" (Mark 7:37, NIV)

Scriptures Relating to Breath and Lungs

"Then the LORD God formed a man from the dust of the ground and breathed into his nostrils the breath of life, and the man became a living being." (Genesis 2:7, NIV)

"In his hand is the life of every creature and the breath of all mankind." (Job 12:10, NIV)

"The Spirit of God has made me; the breath of the Almighty gives me life." (Job 33:4, NIV)

Then he said to me, 'Prophesy to the breath; prophesy, son of man, and say to it, "This is what the Sovereign LORD says: Come, breath, from the four winds and breathe into

these slain, that they may live.'" So I prophesied as he commanded me, and breath entered them; they came to life and
stood up on their feet—a vast army." (Ezekiel 37:9-10, NIV)

"The God who made the world and everything in it is the
Lord of heaven and earth and does not live in temples built
by human hands. And he is not served by human hands, as
if he needed anything. Rather, he himself gives everyone life
and breath and everything else." (Acts 17:24-25, NIV)

Scriptures Relating to the Mind

"You will keep in perfect peace those whose minds are
steadfast, because they trust in you." (Isaiah 26:3, NIV)

"One of them, an expert in the law, tested him with this
question: 'Teacher, which is the greatest commandment in
the Law?' Jesus replied: 'Love the Lord your God with all
your heart and with all your soul and with all your mind.'
This is the first and greatest commandment." (Matthew
22:35-38, NIV)

"The mind governed by the flesh is death, but the mind
governed by the Spirit is life and peace." (Romans 8:6, NIV)

"Therefore, I urge you, brothers and sisters, in view of God's
mercy, to offer your bodies as a living sacrifice, holy and
pleasing to God—this is your true and proper worship.
Do not conform to the pattern of this world, but be trans-
formed by the renewing of your mind. Then you will be
able to test and approve what God's will is—his good, pleasing and perfect will." (Romans 12:1-2, NIV)

"For 'Who has known the mind of the Lord so as to instruct
him?' But we have the mind of Christ. (1 Corinthians 2:16,
NIV)

"Do not be anxious about anything, but in every situation,
by prayer and petition, with thanksgiving, present your

requests to God. And the peace of God, which transcends all understanding, will guard your hearts and your minds in Christ Jesus." (Philippians 4:6-7, NIV)

"You were taught, with regard to your former way of life, to put off your old self, which is being corrupted by its deceitful desires; to be made new in the attitude of your minds." (Ephesians 4:22-23, NIV)

Chapter 9

When Physical Healing Doesn't Come

Some weeks, we see people instantaneously and miraculously healed, and they walk out of our building praising God! On other days, we see that God is beginning to heal the client, but the healing may be more progressive over time. And at other times, some clients don't experience the complete physical healing they so earnestly desire. There are also occasions when clients have received tremendous levels of physical and emotional healing in a physical healing prayer session, only to get sick or have the condition come back again in a few days, weeks, or months later. If and when this happens, it can be troubling to the client—causing doubt, feelings of discouragement, and even disillusionment that God can and will heal long-term.

How should a Christian respond when these things happen? What should be an appropriate Christian response when complete physical healing doesn't come during or after a healing prayer session?

From experience, I have observed that some Christians get angry with God when He doesn't heal. Some people become bitter towards God and blame Him for their physical suffering. They talk as if they have the "right" to healing. Others expect God to automatically heal them and become discouraged and disillusioned when the healing doesn't come. Still others have been told by people in their churches that there must be sin in their life or that they just need to have "more faith," and then they will be healed. This response often results in the sick person blaming themselves and/or carrying around heavy burdens of guilt for not being healed, which can also lead to depression.

Unfortunately, none of the above responses are helpful or productive for long-term spiritual health and growth. They are actually spiritually detrimental and harmful to the soul, and can drive a wedge in a person's relationship with God. If it's discovered that a client has been blamed by another church or healing ministry in the past for their "lack of faith," the Team Leader should offer them encouragement and hope that their physical condition is not their fault (see John 9:1-12 as an example). Sharing words of truth and promises from God's Word can bring tremendous healing to their souls.

Below is a list of healthier, more biblical responses for clients to exhibit if and when complete physical healing doesn't come.

Continue to seek God's healing

If the client has not yet been healed of their condition, they should not grow discouraged or give up. Encourage them to continue asking, pressing in, and seeking *complete* healing. Clients can rest assured that there is nothing wrong with or selfish about fasting and praying persistently for physical healing (it is important to note that some people may have serious medical conditions and it may not be wise or advisable to fast without their doctor's clearance). Jesus Himself taught His disciples, "Ask and it will be given to you; seek and you will find; knock and the door will be opened to you. For everyone who asks receives; he who seeks finds; and to him who knocks the door will be opened" (Matthew 7:7-8). He also told a parable about the power of persistent prayer in Luke 11:5-10. We have learned from Scripture and in this ministry that God often responds to the prayer of faith (see Mark 10:52, Luke 8:48, James 5:15-16). He responds to the faith of the sick person seeking healing and to the faith of family and friends who are praying for and on the sick person's behalf.

Understand that not all healings are instantaneous

Sometimes, when we read the Gospels and the book of Acts, it can lead us to conclude that all healings should occur instantaneously. When Jesus spoke or touched many sick people, the Gospel writers often tell us that they were *immediately healed* (see Matthew 20:34, Mark 1:41-42, 2:12, 10:52, Luke 5:13, 25). However, we tend to forget that even Jesus, the Son of God, had to touch and/or pray with certain people multiple times for them to receive complete healing (see Mark 8:22-26). Thus, we need to remember that not all healings are instantaneous. And we need to be careful not to create false expectations for healing in people's hearts and minds. Some healings are a *process* and occur over a longer period of time. This happens quite frequently with clients who come to Wellsprings of Freedom International. While the healing process begins during their physical healing prayer session, they may not experience complete physical healing until the spiritual/emotional healing is also complete in future freedom sessions.

Trust that God is ultimately in control of the situation

Even though we may not fully understand why God doesn't completely heal, we can trust that He is on the throne. He is still in control and He will sustain us. We can trust that God has a plan and purpose for whatever we are facing. The apostle Paul teaches us from personal experience that God's grace is sufficient for us. It is more than enough to get us through any and every situation. His power can work best in our weakness (2 Corinthians 12:9). So take heart!

Realize that physical healing is a divine mystery

In Scripture, we see that not everyone was healed of their sickness, disease, or physical condition. For example, why did Jesus choose to heal only one paralytic at the pool of Bethesda when a great number of disabled people were lying around (John 5:1-15)? In Mark 6:1-6, we see that there were other times when even Jesus, the Son of God, could not perform any miracles in certain towns and heal all those who were sick, because of the people's lack of faith. Jesus' healing ministry seemed to be limited by the unbelief of the people in some places. Why did the apostle Paul, who performed miracles of healing throughout the book of Acts, have to leave his co-worker, Trophimus, sick in Miletus (2 Timothy 4:20)? Why wasn't he miraculously healed? Why was Paul not able to minister healing to his fellow worker, Epaphroditus, who became ill and almost died (Philippians 2:25-27)? Why did Timothy continue to struggle with stomach ailments and "frequent illnesses" (1 Timothy 5:23)?

Although we diligently search for answers to all of these "why" questions, the reality is that sometimes we just don't know why God heals some and not others this side of heaven. The reasons are unknown to us and it remains a divine mystery. When this happens, we need to humbly recognize that God's ways are not our ways and His thoughts are not our thoughts. They are much higher than ours (Isaiah 55:8-9).

Author Michael Green offers some helpful insight on why not everyone is healed. He comments, "God does not always choose to heal us physically, and perhaps it is as well that He does not. How people would rush to Christianity (and for all the wrong motives) if it carried with it automatic exemption from sickness! What a nonsense it would make of Christian virtues like longsuffering, patience, and endurance if instant whole-ness were available for all the Christian sick! What a wrong impression it would give of salvation if physical wholeness were perfectly realized on earth while spiritual wholeness were partly reserved for heaven! What a very curious thing it would be if God were to decree death for all His children while not allowing illness for any of them!"[1]

Recognize that all healing is God's work, whether it be through natural or supernatural means

While it is our responsibility as Christians to be persistent in praying for healing, God is the one who ultimately determines *how* He will heal. Whether He chooses to heal supernaturally or naturally through modern medicine, all healing comes from God. One form of healing is no more "spiritual" than another. Green explains it this way: "The point is that all healing is God's work. He is able to heal with or without medical means. It is no more 'spiritual' if the healing comes through the laying on of hands and prayer than if it comes through the hospital and drugs."[2] We should give praise to God for each and every healing that is experienced. And we should not discourage Christians from seeing the doctor, taking prescribed medications, and following through with doctor-recommended or scheduled surgeries.

Believe that God can sustain, redeem, and bring something good out of the situation

Why God doesn't heal may remain a divine mystery. But we can rest assured that He can somehow redeem and use even our sickness to bring glory to Him. How God chooses to reveal His power and glory in and through us will be revealed over time. Over and over again, I have seen how the Lord can use sickness and disease (cancer, etc.) as a powerful testimony of God's faithfulness to other believers and nonbelievers alike. Thus, there can be a hidden purpose in some physical illness and conditions.

Humbly accept the truth that a person cannot control the timing or manner of their healing

There have been several occasions when I have encountered clients who *demanded* physical healing from God. They genuinely felt like they had the right to receive physical healing because of all the "good" they had done for God. In their minds, God was somehow indebted to them. Even more disturbing was the fact that God was *expected* to miraculously heal on their terms.

Experiences with clients like this remind me of a story in the Old Testament of a great military commander named Naaman. Naaman was a mighty warrior who fought for the king of Aram, but suffered from a case of leprosy (an infectious skin disease). He longed to be healed from his affliction and sought out the prophet Elisha in hope of being miraculously healed. We read the story from 2 Kings 5 below:

The king of Aram had great admiration for Naaman, the commander of his army, because through him the LORD had given Aram great victories. But though Naaman was a mighty warrior, he suffered from leprosy.[2] At this time Aramean raiders had invaded the land of Israel, and among their captives was a young girl who had been given to Naaman's wife as a maid.[3] One day the girl said to her mistress, "I wish my master would go to see the prophet in Samaria. He would heal him of his leprosy." [4] So Naaman told the king what the young girl from Israel had said.[5] "Go and visit the prophet," the king of Aram told him. "I will send a letter of introduction for you to take to the king of Israel." So Naaman started out, carrying as gifts 750 pounds of silver, 150 pounds of gold, and ten sets of clothing.[6] The letter to the king of Israel said: "With this letter I present my servant Naaman. I want you to heal him of his leprosy."

[7] When the king of Israel read the letter, he tore his clothes in dismay and said, "This man sends me a leper to heal! Am I God,

that I can give life and take it away? I can see that he's just trying to pick a fight with me." [8] But when Elisha, the man of God, heard that the king of Israel had torn his clothes in dismay, he sent this message to him: "Why are you so upset? Send Naaman to me, and he will learn that there is a true prophet here in Israel." [9] So Naaman went with his horses and chariots and waited at the door of Elisha's house. [10] But Elisha sent a messenger out to him with this message: "Go and wash yourself seven times in the Jordan River. Then your skin will be restored, and you will be healed of your leprosy." [11] But Naaman became angry and stalked away. "I thought he would certainly come out to meet me!" he said. "I expected him to wave his hand over the leprosy and call on the name of the LORD his God and heal me! [12] Aren't the rivers of Damascus, the Abana and the Pharpar, better than any of the rivers of Israel? Why shouldn't I wash in them and be healed?" So Naaman turned and went away in a rage.

[13] But his officers tried to reason with him and said, "Sir, if the prophet had told you to do something very difficult, wouldn't you have done it? So you should certainly obey him when he says simply, 'Go and wash and be cured!'" [14] So Naaman went down to the Jordan River and dipped himself seven times, as the man of God had instructed him. And his skin became as healthy as the skin of a young child, and he was healed!

[15] Then Naaman and his entire party went back to find the man of God. They stood before him, and Naaman said, "Now I know that there is no God in all the world except in Israel. So please accept a gift from your servant." [16] But Elisha replied, "As surely as the LORD lives, whom I serve, I will not accept any gifts." And though Naaman urged him to take the gift, Elisha refused. [17] Then Naaman said, "All right, but please allow me to load two of my mules with earth from this place, and I will take it back home with me. From now on I will never again offer burnt offerings or sacrifices to any other god except the LORD. (2 Kings 5:1-17, NLT)

It is clear that Naaman had false expectations in his mind as to when, where, and how he would be healed. Upon arriving at the prophet Elisha's house, Naaman did not particularly care for Elisha's messenger's instructions to wash in the Jordan River seven times. He seemed offended that he was asked to wash himself in the Jordan River, instead of in the rivers of Damascus. Perhaps he was also offended that Elisha himself did not come out to greet and speak with him. It says that Naaman became angry and went away in a rage. Naaman declared, "I thought that he [Elisha] would surely come out to me and stand and call on the name of the LORD his God, wave his hand over the spot and cure me of my leprosy" (5:11, NIV). He expected the miraculous and was not impressed with the mundane. He expected the dramatic, only to be disappointed by the dull and ordinary. In Naaman's mind, his healing wasn't supposed to be like this. It was supposed to be much more sensational and impressive.

Interestingly, Naaman's officers tried to reason with him (5:13). Why wouldn't he want to do something so simple to be cleansed and healed of this humiliating disease? Why would he want to continue suffering when he had a prime opportunity to be healed? In the end, Naaman decided to humble himself and do what the prophet had asked him to do. As a result, Naaman was completely and miraculously healed. His flesh was restored and his skin became as healthy as the skin of a young child (5:14).

We can learn several important truths from Naaman's story. First of all, the reality is that we cannot control the time and place of our healing. Nor can we control the manner by which we are healed. We cannot demand healing from God nor do we get to set the terms and conditions for our healing. God is certainly not obligated to heal us or to heal us the way we want. Neither can we envision in our minds how and when we will be healed. Why? Because healing is not under our control. It's ultimately under God's control. It's for Him alone to decide. He is the Sovereign One and we are His humble servants. It's never the other way around.[3]

In his book on spiritual gifts, David K. Bernard offers some wise advice for those struggling to understand God's sovereignty in the healing process. He writes:

"We should pray for a sick person's healing, and we have assurance that God will hear and answer this prayer—but in His manner and time, not necessarily ours. He may heal instantly, He may begin a gradual process of healing. He may use whatever we consider 'natural' means, He may heal later, He may give grace through a time of sickness, or He may allow the person to die in faith and receive the answer in the resurrection. There can be many reasons why God does not heal instantly; some we can discern, while others are known only to the sovereign mind of God."[4]

Second, we should not get angry with God when He doesn't heal the way we want Him to or expect Him to. Naaman's reaction to Elisha's instructions was a prideful and arrogant response. Naaman thought he knew better as to how God should heal him. Filled with anger, he went off in a rage and almost missed out on a miracle. In order to receive God's healing, Naaman needed to come to a place of surrender and assume a posture of humility before God and His servant. Healing begins when we come to the end of ourselves, release God from our own false expectations, and repent of any anger or bitterness that we may be holding against Him. The truth is that we have no right to be angry at God when He operates in ways that are beyond our own understanding and/or expectations. He is God and we are not. Therefore, our only response is to surrender and trust that He is good, that He is for us and not against us, and that He hears the cries of our hearts.

Finally, we cannot manipulate God or purchase our healing with money and gifts. In 2 Kings 5:4-6, we read how the king of Aram told Naaman to go and visit the king of Israel. The king of

Aram sent along with Naaman 750 pounds of silver, 150 pounds of gold, and ten sets of new clothing as gifts. He even wrote a personal letter for Naaman to take to the king of Israel, thinking that would be enough to persuade the king to heal Naaman of his leprosy. Upon reading the letter, the king of Israel tore his robes in dismay and said, "This man sends me a leper to heal! Am I God, that I can give life and take it away?" (5:7a).

This story reminds us that no human being has the power to heal. Nor can God be manipulated, bribed, or coerced into healing. Healing cannot be purchased for a price. Both the king of Israel and the prophet Elisha understood this truth. Even after Naaman was healed, the prophet Elisha refused to accept Naaman's generous gifts (5:16). The power to heal comes from God alone. We cannot bargain with God for healing.

Endnotes

1 Michael Green. *I Believe In The Holy Spirit* (Grand Rapids, MI: Eerdmans Publishing, 2004), Location 2558.

2 Green, Location 2550.

3 Bill Johnson & Randy Clark. *Healing Unplugged: Conversations and Insights from Two Veteran Healing Leaders* (Grand Rapids, MI: Chosen Books, 2012), p. XXX

4 David K. Bernard. *Spiritual Gifts: A practical study with inspirational accounts of God's sSupernatural gGifts tTo His church* (Hazelwood, MO: (???)Word Aflame Press, 1997), Location 1896.

Physical Healing Prayer Session

CLIENT NAME: _____ DATE: _____

Team Leader: _____

Team Members: _____

Prayer Request(s): _____

_____

_____

_____

_____

Healing: _____

_____

_____

_____

_____

Recommended Follow-Up:

❏ Please call the client to schedule a full 3-hour freedom session.

❏ Client will call if they decide they want further ministry.

❏ No more sessions are needed at this time.

Notes: _____

_____

_____

_____

_____

FOR OFFICE USE:
Session #: _____
Splashes
Consent
Minor Consent

Team Leader Signature: _____

Appendix B: Personal Consent and Liability Waiver Form

Personal Consent and Liability Waiver

Name _____ Phone _____

Address _____

City _____ State _____ Zip _____

Email _____

_____ *I would like to receive the Wellsprings of Freedom monthly e-newsletter.*

I do hereby affirm and state that I,

_____ ,

(Print your name here)

give my consent for a Wellsprings of Freedom Team to minister to me in the areas of biblical counseling, inner healing, and the ministry of deliverance and/or physical healing. I understand and acknowledge that all team members, professional ministers or trained volunteers, involved in this ministry are not licensed or trained as psychotherapists, mental health professionals, or professional counselors.

All guidance, counsel, and advice that I receive will be solely based on scriptural principles and Christian biblical standards as spelled out in the Holy Bible, the written Word of God.

I further understand and acknowledge that all ministry is under the direction and control of the Holy Spirit, and that no guarantees are made, nor can be made, with regard to my healing and/or deliverance.

I state that I have voluntarily sought this ministry for myself and that I hereby release Wellsprings of Freedom International, and all volunteers working with the Wellsprings of Freedom Ministry, from any and all claims of actual or implied liability that may arise now or in the future as a result of the ministry I receive.

Signed:_____ Date: _____

Appendix C: Parental Consent and Liability Waiver Form

Parental Consent & Liability Form

I do hereby affirm and state that my child,

_____ ,

(Print CHILD's name here)

has been given my consent for a Wellsprings of Freedom Team to minister to him/her in the areas of biblical counseling, inner healing, and the ministry of deliverance and/or physical healing. I understand and acknowledge that all team members, professional ministers or trained volunteers, involved in this ministry are not licensed or trained as psychotherapists, mental health professionals, or professional counselors.

All guidance, counsel, and advice that I receive will be solely based on scriptural principles and Christian biblical standards as spelled out in the Holy Bible, the written Word of God.

I further understand and acknowledge that all ministry is under the direction and control of the Holy Spirit, and that no guarantees are made, nor can be made, with regard to my healing and/or deliverance.

I state that I have voluntarily sought this ministry for myself and my child and that I hereby release Wellsprings of Freedom International, and all volunteers working with the Wellsprings of Freedom Ministry, from any and all claims of actual or implied liability that may arise now or in the future as a result of the ministry I receive.

Signed:_____ Date: _____

Parent Name:_____

Address: _____

City/State/Zip:_____

Phone: _____ Email: _____

Bibliography

Bernard, David K. *Spiritual Gifts: A Practical Study With Inspirational Accounts of God's Supernatural Gifts To His Church.* (Hazelwood, MO: (???)Word Aflame Press, 1997).

Blue, Ken. *Authority To Heal.* (Downers Grove, IL: InterVarsity Press, 1987).

Bock, Darrell L. NIV *Application Commentary, New Testament: Luke.* (Grand Rapids, MI: Zondervan, 1996).

Burge, Gary M. NIV *Application Commentary, New Testament: John.* (Grand Rapids, MI: Zondervan, 2000).

Fee, Gordon D. *The First Epistle to the Corinthians (NICNT).* (Grand Rapids, MI: Eerdmans Publishing: Grand Rapids, MI, 1987).

Green, Michael. *I Believe In The Holy Spirit.* (Grand Rapids, MI: Eerdmans Publishing, 2004).

Gundry, Stanley N. & Wayne A. Grudem. *Are Miraculous Gifts For Today? Four Views.* (Grand Rapids, MI: (Zondervan, 2011).

Johnson, Bill & Randy Clark. *Healing Unplugged: Conversations and Insights from Two Veteran Healing Leaders.* (Grand Rapids, MI: Chosen Books, 2012).

Ladd, George Elton. *The Gospel of the Kingdom: Scriptural Studies in the Kingdom of God.* (Grand Rapids, MI: Eerdmans Publishing, 1959).

MacMullen, Ramsay. *Christianizing The Roman Empire (A.D. 100-400).* (New York and London: Yale University Press, 1984).

MacNutt, Francis. *The Healing Reawakening: Reclaiming Our Lost Inheritance.* (Grand Rapids, MI: Chosen Books, 2005).

MacNutt, Francis. *Healing (Revised and Expanded).* (Notre Dame, IN: Ave Maria Press, 1999).

Nystrom, David P. NIV *Application Commentary, New Testament: James*. (Grand Rapids, MI: Zondervan, 1997).

Spangler, Ann. *The Names of God*. (Grand Rapids, MI: Zondervan, 2009).

Talbert, Charles H. *Reading Luke: A Literary and Theological Commentary on the Third Gospel*. (Macon, GA: Smyth & Helwys Publishing, 2013).

Venter, Alexander F. *Doing Healing: How to Minister God's Healing in the Power of the Spirit*. (Cape Town, South Africa: Vineyard International Publishing, 2009).

Wagner, C. Peter. *Discover Your Spiritual Gifts: Updated & Expanded*. (Ventura, CA: Regal Books, 2005).

Wilkins, Michael J. NIV *Application Commentary, New Testament: Matthew*. (Grand Rapids, MI: Zondervan, 2004).

Wimber, John & Kevin Springer. *Power Healing*. (New York City: HarperOne, 1987).

About the Authors

Rev. Brian S. Burke was born in Staten Island, NY and has been actively involved in healing and freedom ministry since 2006. Brian is an ordained pastor in The Wesleyan Church and is a graduate of Indiana Wesleyan University (Marion, IN) and Wheaton College Graduate School (Wheaton, IL). Brian, his wife Cara, and their family served as cross-cultural missionaries in Russia for twelve years with Global Partners. While serving as the Mission Director and giving leadership to the mission work in Russia, Brian and his wife established a Wellsprings of Freedom International team in Vladimir, Russia, and he has led nearly 2,000 freedom sessions over the last decade. Since 2013, Brian has been serving full-time as the Executive Vice President of Global Ministry for Wellsprings of Freedom International in Rock Island, IL. He is also the co-author of *With Gentle Authority: A Manual for Inner Healing and Freedom Ministry*, the WFI *Training Module Notebook*, and serves as one of the main contributing authors to the "Splashes From Wellsprings" discipleship website (www.splashesfromwellsprings.com).

Lynette Johnson was born in Geneseo, IL and has been actively involved with inner healing and freedom ministry for thirteen years, serving as an Intercessor on two freedom teams. In 2013, Lynette helped develop and lead two physical healing prayer teams a week. Over the past thirteen years, she has served in over 1,000 freedom sessions and 200 physical healing prayer sessions, and has been on fifteen mission trips with Wellsprings of Freedom International. She formerly worked as an RN staff nurse for twenty-three years working on a skilled/long-term care unit. She has one daughter and son-in-law, five grandchildren, and six great grandchildren.

Looking for more information on how to be equipped and empowered for spiritual battle? Check out these two resources available from Wellsprings of Freedom International!

Introducing "Splashes from Wellsprings"
www.splashesfromwellsprings.com

We love and value our clients and want them to experience deep levels of freedom at all times. For this reason, we have created an exciting online resource called "Splashes from Wellsprings." "Splashes" is a discipleship website that offers a vast array of information to help clients as they prepare for their sessions, go through sessions, and then learn how to walk in their freedom. It contains over 260 articles, over 100 miracle stories, and frequently asked questions, as well as books for recommended reading. All this and more awaits you on this website. The cost to purchase a membership is only $16.95 per month, and it allows WFI to continue to pay forward the blessing of offering freedom to a broken world!

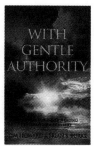

With Gentle Authority
by Tim Howard & Brian S. Burke

Are you looking for a resource that will be a practical guide to better equip your church to do inner healing and freedom ministry in a gentle, yet powerful way? *With Gentle Authority* is our comprehensive training manual designed to give you the answers you are seeking. With over twenty-five years of combined experience, the authors will walk you through why this type of ministry is needed in the local church today and how to do freedom ministry in your location. You can purchase *With Gentle Authority* from our website at www.wellspringsoffreedom.com or in e-book format from Amazon.com.